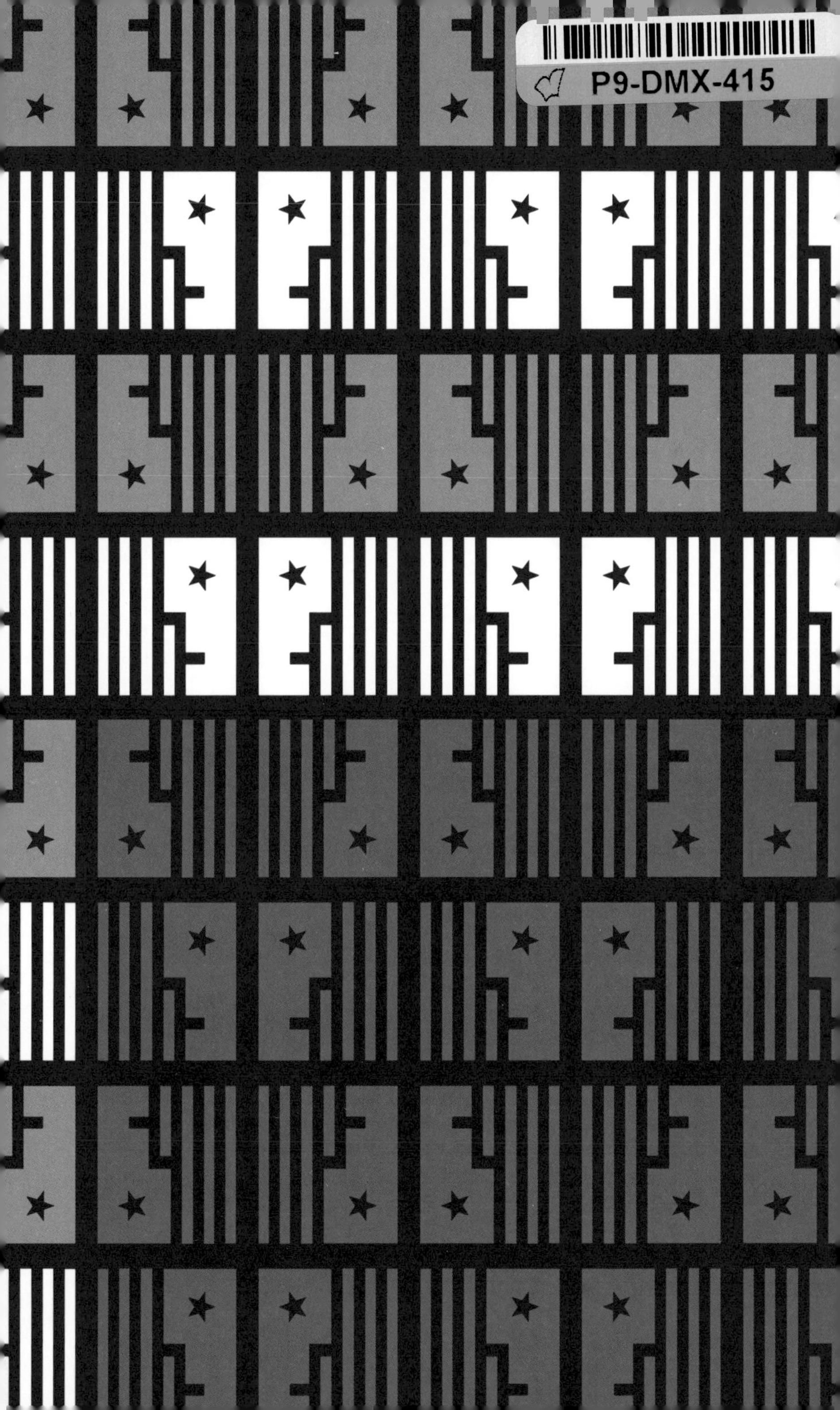

My Brother Moochie

My Brother Moochie

Regaining Dignity
in the Face of
Crime, Poverty, and Racism
in the American South

★ ★ ★

Issac J. Bailey

Other Press
New York

Production editor: Yvonne E. Cárdenas
Text designer: Julie Fry
This book was set in Berndal by Alpha Design & Composition
of Pittsfield, NH.

10 9 8 7 6 5 4 3 2 1

Printed in the United States of America on acid-free paper. For information write to Other Press LLC, 267 Fifth Avenue, 6th Floor, New York, NY 10016. Or visit our Web site: www.otherpress.com

Library of Congress Cataloging-in-Publication Data

Names: Bailey, Issac J., author.
Title: My brother Moochie : regaining dignity in the face of crime, poverty, and racism in the American South / Issac J. Bailey.
Description: New York : Other Press, [2018]
Identifiers: LCCN 2017049799 | ISBN 9781590518601 (hardcover) | ISBN 9781590518618 (ebook)
Subjects: LCSH: Bailey, Issac J. | African American men—Family relationships—Biography. | African American prisoners—Biography. | African American families—Biography. | Criminal justice, Administration of—United States. | Crime—Sociological aspects.
Classification: LCC E185.86 .B2525 2018 | DDC 306.85/08996073—dc23
LC record available at https://lccn.loc.gov/2017049799

Dedicated to Moochie, Sherrie, Doug, Willie, Josh, Mel, Jody, Zadoc, James, Jordan, Mama, Boss, Aunt Doretha.

We are still here; we still have a lot to offer this world.

My Brother Moochie

Monsters

> All my life I had been looking for something, and everywhere I turned someone tried to tell me what it was. I accepted their answers, too, though they were often in contradiction and even self-contradictory. I was naive. I was looking for myself and asking everyone except myself questions which I, and only I, could answer.
>
> —Ralph Ellison, *Invisible Man*

I held my thirteen-year-old son's chin between the index finger and thumb of my right hand, squeezing and lifting it ever so slightly to make sure our eyes locked. Our faces were so close I'm sure he could smell my breath, feel the spittle from my mouth.

"I can't tell you how angry I am," I told him in a barely audible voice. If I yelled, I knew I'd lose control.

He was nearly my height and athletic, a nationally ranked high jumper and middle-distance sprinter. I was still built like the football player I had been a couple of decades earlier. I wanted him to feel that physical difference like he never had.

"I can't *tell* you how *angry* I am right now," I repeated.

The slightest tear began welling up in the corner of Kyle's right eye. I let his chin go and left him alone in his bedroom, though, sadly, not because of what I had almost done, but because I wanted to do something more to cause *real* tears, because I wanted to ignore that my wife, Tracy, told me hitting him would be wrong, and ineffective, because I wanted to literally shake maturity right into him—because I so desperately wanted to save him from...I'm not even quite sure what. All I had caught him doing was being a teenager, being less than honest with me one too many times, letting his grades slip a little, arming himself with a more defiant attitude as if to announce his newly discovered manhood to the world. Still, he's well on his way to becoming a better man than I'll ever be. And yet, my instinct was to crush his soul to save his black body from some undetermined future harm that may never materialize.

He was born in 2001, the year researchers said we crossed a Rubicon, when fully a third of young black men Kyle's age were projected to end up behind bars if we didn't make significant changes in the way we treat them, and how they treat themselves. It wasn't that statistic that scared me, though. It was what I had long known, and why when Tracy and I decided to have kids, I initially wanted a girl.

I was afraid of black boys. The image of them was everything I didn't want to be.

The shameful truth is that a not insignificant part of my mind had so thoroughly absorbed the ugly myths about black boys, I seriously wondered if violent behavior was the result of an immutable genetic reality unique to those born black and male like me.

I was a black boy who grew up with eight black brothers, and a nephew raised like a brother, along with two black sisters. While researchers might turn out to be right, and a full third of young black men might end up in jail or prison at some point in their lives, it's already been worse for us. Half of the black boys in my immediate family ended up behind bars. I spent much of my early parenting years trying to deny that the shame of that reality had any effect on my treatment of my only son. I was lying to myself.

I knew it almost instantly when I walked out of Kyle's room and downstairs and remembered the years-long debate within my family about why some of us went astray. Half of my family seems convinced our disparate outcomes resulted from my mother's decision to not beat the youngest, those who got into the most trouble, the way she had beaten the rest of us. That belief is rooted in how black people were treated as slaves in the American South and the Bible most black people—nearly 80 percent of black Americans self-identify as Christian, more than any other group in a nation in which religious identity is undergoing a transformation—read and swear by. I can't count the number of times I heard the words "black people!" in exasperation at the sight of another black boy who dropped out of school or a black man milling around at the park with a tall can of Schlitz Malt Liquor in a brown paper bag. They weren't individuals who had made wrecks of their lives or succumbed to overwhelming challenges; they were representations of the black race. That's the way many of us spoke about struggling black men. Even in the black churches I attended, Father's Day was used more often as a scolding for deadbeat dads than a celebration of fathers working twelve-hour shifts in a nearby factory to keep the lights on.

I never said such things out loud. But it doesn't mean I didn't grow up believing them, too. Deep into adulthood, I thought I was one of the progressive ones—until I almost beat my son for no good reason. About a week after the encounter with Kyle, a cop in a South Carolina high school made national news for assaulting a black teenage girl who had refused to put away her cell phone. He threw her around as though tossing trash in a Dumpster. I was horrified and outraged and argued with anyone who tried to deflect attention from what that officer did.

"No, she was not the problem, it was the adults," I said loudly. "She did what teenagers since the Stone Age have done, get under the skin of adults."

What I didn't say is that too many black parents treat their kids the way that cop treated that teenage girl, with a kind of desperate hatred born of a warped sense of love. I'm not just referring to extreme corporal punishment, the kind on display during the Baltimore riots when a black mom was deemed heroic for being caught on TV wailing on her wayward son. It's also because despite our loud protestations, many of us don't think we've been fully accepted in this still largely white-dominated society. Unruly, nappy-headed kids in our midst make us think we never will. That's why so many of us are more comfortable when our kids fit, rather than reinvent, the mold.

We are willing to beat our children to near death if that's what it takes to get to a successful adulthood. When they step out of line, we first wonder if we spared the rod too much, not if we didn't give enough hugs. We are willing to call them the ugliest names, label them as thugs, see them as monsters, likely out of an effort to prove to others that, yes, we, too, believe in personal responsibility; we, too, can do right and be right and worthy of their respect.

Before that awful day with my son, here's what I had done to prove I was one of the proverbial good black people: I married Tracy Swinton. We took precautions to not have kids before we were ready. We bought a house, then planned to bring kids into our world. We decided we wouldn't be working full-time jobs simultaneously because we wanted a lead parent home with our children. That decision caused us financial stress—it got so bad we had to dig out coins from between the couch cushions to buy gasoline—but we thought it was the right thing to do.

We worked hard to advance in our careers, me as a journalist, Tracy as an educator and consultant who earned a doctorate in education and founded a nonprofit literacy program to help at-risk kids. We joined a church, did community work, kept our kids in the presence of good influences. We volunteered in the schools and showed up for performances and parent-teacher conferences. We monitored their homework and responded every time a teacher had a report, good or bad. We cheered at their sporting events, provided incentives to keep them inspired, implemented various forms of discipline—took away privileges, instituted earlier bedtimes, unleashed a plastic ruler on an open palm—and hugged them and told them we loved them, that we expected great things from them because they could accomplish just about anything they wanted. And despite all of that, I was standing in my son's room believing hurting him was the way to save him from dangers that had yet to manifest.

I wasn't only angry. I was hurt, disappointed. Terrified. All parents are afraid for their children. My fear was deeper, because no matter how much I've tried to leave it behind, the stereotypical image of the violent black boy who deserves to have been shot down in the street by a cop or forced to rot away in solitary confinement never leaves me. It doesn't matter that I've studied the issue for the past two decades and can cite study after study about the myth of such an image, about how implicit and overt bias continue fueling it, about how black boys, and black girls, start off at a disadvantage because of the historical realities that accompany them and their skin wherever they go.

I'm scared for Kyle in a way many black parents are scared for their kids. I suspect, though, that white parents don't wonder about the pathology of their race no matter how many times white boys shoot up elementary schools or movie theaters. Many black parents, like most black people I've ever known, grimace every time a mug shot of a black boy shows up on the TV news or in the local paper, because they know the image of yet another black boy doing something awful suggests something awful about them.

We aren't just parenting and suffering the silent second-guessing that affects everyone who has ever tried to raise a teenager. We are still trying to prove our worth. And because we don't realize that's a large portion of our motivation, our children take it on the chin.

We lament that society doesn't allow them to just be kids, to work their way through the stupid things we all did as kids. But we don't allow them to be just that, either. Their talking back to the teacher isn't just typical teen defiance that's been with us since man began communicating and needs to be dealt with proportionately; it's evidence that we, as a people, have failed, that they are making us look bad, as a race. In our quiet moments, we find it hard to believe what should be obvious, that at-risk black boys who find in gangs stability and love they couldn't find elsewhere, for whatever reason, are just following a natural pattern seen in all groups of young people who feel alienated and left behind. Instead, we beat ourselves up emotionally, which is why we tolerate so much of the harm—physical, psychic, emotional—that others continuously unleash upon them.

Because of that, black Americans are connected in a way white people aren't. It is a progressive conceit that race matters less today, but when a Tamir Rice is shot, many, if not most, black parents cringe because he wore the same skin our children do, and we know that skin played a significant role in his death. Because of that, families like mine feel a double dose of shame that separates us even from other black families. We are the black sheep of the black sheep. We are the source of black embarrassment, the poker that stirs the embers of black shame. We are the seed of truth supplying sustenance to the stereotype. We didn't hold up our end of the bargain in the respectability game.

As a member of the perpetrator's family, that's why you don't know what you are allowed to feel, or think. Victims can mourn, and others will help them mourn. When prosecutors and pundits talk about justice, they are referring to victims and their families, not families like mine. Why should anybody give a damn that the ripple effects of crime change our lives, too? We don't get to mourn. We don't get to reflect, at least not fully, not publicly.

To stand by a man you love after he has done something dastardly is to be accused of having a lack of respect for what the victim has endured. To demand that he not be known solely by his worst act is to be accused of excusing evil. To not be there for him would feel like a dereliction of familial duty, a betrayal of the worst order. To state the truth—that sentencing him to a long stay behind bars would be a devastating blow to your family—is to open yourself up to ridicule and screams of, "He should have thought about that before he decided to kill a man."

There are no good options for families like mine. Navigating the internal struggle and external pressure becomes an impossibility. Shame gives way to a self-imposed silence that makes seeking, or receiving, potentially life-altering help less likely by the day.

We let other black and marginalized people down, made it harder for them to get a fair hearing, because there's shame that comes with being forced to walk around in dark skin in a society built upon the demonization of dark skin. Then there's the shame that comes from the realization that we have committed acts pundits and politicians have used to either justify that demonization or declare that their fear of those who look like us is warranted. White supremacists and white nationalists aren't our friends, but they love having us around. Our mistakes make it easier for them to sell their lies about pathological black violence.

Potential allies speak of us in hushed tones, if at all, while proudly pushing for humane criminal justice reform for nonviolent offenders and those who love them. Forcefully arguing in favor of similar consideration for families like mine is just too risky.

We are the nightmare, not the hope, of the slave.

That's how it feels to be on this side of the criminal justice system. We are the rightly convicted, not the unjustly accused. We've done things David Duke has long said black people would if given the chance.

That's why I've been afraid of myself for as long as I've known myself. Fortunately, I haven't known myself very long, because I didn't always know that I was capable of murder. Neither did I know you didn't have to find your way to a battlefield as an adult to suffer post-traumatic stress disorder. All you had to do was be born into the middle of a war, have your nine-year-old eyes watch helplessly as your oldest brother is taken away in handcuffs and your thirty-five-year-old brain later produce overpowering images of you doing to your wife and kids what your brother did to the man whose life he took.

★ ★ ★

I thought about murdering my wife. I don't know why I didn't kill her. Not knowing what stopped me haunts me more than the shame that came with ever having harbored such thoughts.

I'd get up in the morning and squeeze my eyes shut in the shower as the warm water made its way down my body while visions of my wife's bloodied body flooded my mind, picking up where they left off the day before. Sometimes they would come in the form of nightmares scaring me awake in the middle of the night. Sometimes they would have me kicking and screaming in my sleep until Tracy would shake me from their grip. Mostly they waited until I could see and process everything around me.

I'd take a deep breath, say a quick prayer, hope my heart would stop pounding so loudly, get dressed. I'd hug Lyric, my only daughter, maybe tap Kyle on the head before kissing Tracy softly on the lips—I vowed to never leave the house without a kiss from her—walk out the front door and hop into my blue Ford Explorer Sport Trac. Usually within the first three minutes of my twenty-minute drive to the office, I'd begin the routine anew, squeezing my eyes tight even while approaching stoplights and stop signs and making my way onto one of our area's busiest stretches of highway. That's when I'd start violently thrusting my head from side to side, again and again and again, hard enough to feel as though my brain was banging against my skull. I played football for ten years. Not one hit on the field had ever made my head feel that way.

I'd pull into the parking lot of *The Sun News*, shut off the engine, take another long, slow deep breath and make my way into the newsroom, but not before plastering a smile on my face. For years, such was my life. I told no one. Not Tracy, not my family, not friends. No one.

I had to battle those demons two, maybe three, times every week. The visions, in various forms, had been with me for as long as I can remember. They weren't always of Tracy. Sometimes they were of my children. Before marrying, I'd see my own mangled, bloodied body in a ditch after a car accident or being impaled or gang raped in prison. That is when I wasn't imagining others in similar scenes. The visions grew in intensity and frequency as the years grew long, gradually wearing away my ability to keep them at bay.

The most powerful of them were of Tracy and my kids. There were times I excused myself from the house in the middle of the afternoon because those visions would try to convince me to pick up a knife. That's when I finally had to make a choice, abandon Tracy, Kyle, and Lyric to protect them from their husband and father, or ask for help.

I decided to tell my wife I had been thinking about killing her. She didn't run. Years later she said she didn't process the magnitude of what I was saying, particularly given what she knew about my family's history. She took it seriously enough to demand I see a psychiatrist, something she had long wanted me to do anyway. She had never been convinced I had fully grappled with the demons of which she was aware. She knew having my hero big brother, Moochie, serve a life sentence for first-degree murder remained a central theme in my life. She knew the emotional and psychological effects of a severe stutter that worsened when

Moochie was taken away and had accompanied me into adulthood.

I set up an appointment with a psychiatrist recommended through work and scheduled the roughly dozen one-hour sessions around my reporting schedule. I'd spend hours in the morning and early afternoon interviewing the mothers and siblings of young black people (mostly men) who had been shot dead or severely harmed. I'd then steal away for an hour to privately talk to a short white woman about the violence I had witnessed and experienced growing up.

That's the first time someone told me I could be suffering from PTSD. Twenty-five years had passed since my oldest brother, Moochie, had killed a white man named James Bunch. It was the first time in a quarter of a century I was unspooling those memories, or some distorted remnants of them, with another human being. During that process, my psychiatrist became convinced I was a PTSD sufferer, and maybe that's why even though I was there the night Moochie ran home in bloody clothes, I have never been able to *see* that night again in my mind's eye, no matter how hard I try.

The diagnosis was a relief, and a burden. Though they never left me, the visions began to subside. Every time I resisted the urge to try to shake them out of my head, they lost potency. My smile became more genuine. I no longer lived in an emotional straitjacket. I started feeling things again, beyond fear, beyond shame, beyond regret. I was happy in a way I had never been.

It wasn't long, though, until my newfound joy made way for another revelation. There's no worse feeling than coming to grips with the reality that you were potentially the biggest threat facing your family. But there's one that comes close: trying to process how to love a hero big brother who had murdered and younger brothers who ended up doing awful things as well.

I wasn't the only person in my family who had witnessed what I had, who had lived through the aftermath of a murder and watching a pillar of our household taken away in chains and shackles. The effects of a murder from 1982, and the cumulative effects of other crimes I witnessed while growing up, were still influencing my behavior, darkening my thoughts. What had they been doing to the hearts and minds of my siblings? Had so many of us ended up in prison because of those repercussions?

I didn't know if any of them had been suffering PTSD, too (most people exposed to the violence I was aren't later diagnosed with the disorder), didn't know in what other form the ripple effects were showing up in their heads, if at all. All I knew was that if it could grab hold of me and not let go for twenty-five years, it could have done the same to them. That realization helped me square the circle that is my knowledge of them, smart, engaging, compassionate men I knew would sacrifice themselves to protect me and others they loved but who, nonetheless, committed horrifically stupid and even evil acts against others.

★ ★ ★

I stopped being ashamed of my brothers for the killings they committed or were complicit in when I owned up to my own struggles against violent thoughts and urges. I was too ashamed of myself to remain ashamed of them. That's why I know not every bad act can be prevented; human behavior is too hard to predict. But a well-timed smile from a stranger can unknowingly prevent a crime. A caring adult providing an unearned second chance to the wayward black boy instead of condemnation can unknowingly prevent crime. Well-thought-out interventions that reach into the lives of children in distress—literacy programs like the one founded by my wife that put a child on a path previously unavailable—have done the same.

Such underappreciated acts of crime prevention make our communities safer. They also make it harder for nonprofit executive directors, researchers, and kind strangers to prove the effectiveness of their actions. There's no way to count the number of crimes prevented by the well-timed smile or during the ninety minutes spent reading with other kids and volunteering in a community center instead of having them wander along unforgiving, unkind streets. The line between a murder and a preserved life is thinner than many like to believe. But I know. My brothers taught me. The visions invading my mind made sure I'd never forget.

That's why I felt stuck inside a recurring loop of violent images. It feels as though PTSD was my mind's way of rendering me guilty of the sin of having been born into a family that includes men who had beaten their wives and killed other men. I saw a similar struggle in the black mothers I interviewed about how their children had been killed.

They'd tell me tales of nightclub shoot-outs, wasted talent, hope baptized by blood. A mother told me about her son who had been killed during a drug deal gone bad. They shot him in the back of the head. They drove his body and SUV deep into the woods and that mother's son spent weeks rotting away in the Southern summer sun. She was forced to appraise preserved remains carefully unrolled and placed under a microscope by the medical examiner, reduced to examining a rotting piece of tattooed skin to identify her son. He was a young black man killed by other young black men. They were participants in an illegal drug trade my youngest brothers had become expert in a couple of counties away.

That black mother had been reduced to tears and heartache, regret and anger. And shame. I knew her shame because I knew my shame. It is the shame shared by black people who know the sting of murder and prison bars, and those who don't but know that their dark skin connects them to those who do.

That kind of shame is debilitating. My shame feels even more shameful. It runs layers deep because I spent many years thinking what many Americans think but dare not acknowledge publicly, that a white life violently taken is tragic, a black one routine. It's why I unintentionally placed the humanity of the white victims of my family above the black victims. I know I'm not alone because nearly half of black people find it easier to associate black faces and negative labels (about 80 percent of white people do as well) than white faces and negative words on implicit bias tests created by researchers at Harvard University. I know I'm not alone because black men are more likely to receive harsher sentences for committing similar crimes as white men, according to a study in the journal *Criminology* and the *Yale Law Journal,* among others. Killers are more likely to receive the death penalty when they take a white life than a black one, according to a large body of data, including that compiled by Amnesty International and many others. The Marshall Project reported that white people who kill black people often face little to no legal consequences, while a black person who kills a white person—under any circumstances—almost never escapes a reckoning with the criminal justice system.

When I was a young boy, I lamented that the first of my brothers to enter the world murdered a white man with a knife. On the back end, I wondered if I had done enough to support my youngest brother, given that he'd committed a myriad of felonies that could land him in a federal prison for the rest of his life, or the brother and nephew who were already in state prisons, or the brother who no longer is.

That's why shame has been my constant companion for as long as I can remember. I've long known that violence can happen to and be committed by good people, that conjuring up boogeymen to explain an imperfect world is for the privileged, not men like me. That's why the visions of killing the woman I love and the children we created scared me so much I considered leaving them. I didn't know where I'd go, if I'd leave a note, or call Tracy once I had reached my unknown destination. I'd drive my old truck to a hotel somewhere in Myrtle Beach, or maybe a few hours away in Charleston to the south or Charlotte to the north, check in and do... I don't know what. All I knew was that the blood running through the veins of my imprisoned brothers was also coursing through mine.

That's why the visions felt real. All the intellect in the world couldn't overcome the power they held over me. How could I square the commonly believed image of me—the strong one, the one who'd never succumb to the temptation of evil—with thoughts about hurting those I love the most? That's why I was never at peace, no matter how hard or how long I smiled. The visions were worst when I did my best work, which meant telling stories about young black drug dealers looking for real jobs to leave the game because they were emotionally and physically exhausted from the nonstop secrecy and running; about young black drug dealers leaving the streets and reporting back to me that something I said had convinced them to change their lives; about those who ended up dead or in prison despite my efforts at mentorship; about the nuance that too often gets lost in discussions about so-called black-on-black crime.

★ ★ ★

I've been a journalist for two decades. During much of that time, I've used my research, interviewing, and writing skills to challenge a mostly white and conservative readership to look at race and crime through a new lens. It took me a while to muster the courage, but I began using my family's story to drive home the point that black men who commit crimes were just as complex and worthy of respect as their imperfect white children. I thought I had done a great service, even publicly unmasking the racial stereotypes deeply rooted in my own brain, until I realized they were pocketing my goodwill while refusing to commit to the hard, internal work necessary for long-term change. The tipping point came when a man named George Zimmerman killed a boy named Trayvon Martin, a black boy with a baby face like my son's baby face.

It was Zimmerman with the past run-ins with the police, for fighting a cop and being accused of domestic abuse by a former girlfriend. But it was Trayvon who was labeled the thug. It was the decision by the police in Sanford, Florida, that turned a tragedy into a national flash point. The police department decided not to fully pursue an investigation, decided to ignore a detective who believed Zimmerman was a liar, decided to let Zimmerman go after killing a black boy as though all he had done was accidentally run over an alley cat.

And still, my initial reaction was that though a full investigation was warranted, no one should forget that black boys like Trayvon were more likely to be killed by other black boys. I knew more black boys who had killed and hurt black boys than I had known men like Zimmerman. My focus changed when the white people around me—even the parents of children Trayvon's age, even those I had spent years worshipping with in the same church—began calling Trayvon a thug, too, began blaming him for having been murdered. They didn't care that all he was doing was walking home from the store with a fruity drink and candy in his hands, didn't care that he belonged in that neighborhood with his father and his father's partner, didn't care that he ran away from Zimmerman when he saw the strange man following him, didn't care that he wasn't armed and had every right to defend himself from a man stalking him in a van at night.

They sided with the killer. They empathized with the killer. They prioritized the killer's supposed fear over Trayvon's dead black body.

Trayvon had done nothing wrong. Zimmerman did everything wrong. And yet, the people whom I had broken bread with in their homes, they in mine, sided with the man who put a bullet in a black boy's chest. A now-former friend insisted Zimmerman had every reason to be afraid of Trayvon because black boys are more likely to commit violent crime than others.

"But what about Kyle?" I asked him. "He's a young black man. Is it logical to be afraid of him, too?"

"Of course not," he assured me. "I know *your* son."

It became clear that too many white people were expert at loving and respecting individual black people while stubbornly holding fast to stereotypes about black people. I was angry at them for so callously disregarding the murder of a black boy—and at myself for having played an unwitting role in allowing them to be comfortable in their callousness.

I felt more shame than anger. I had spent nearly two decades in a mostly white, conservative Southern church believing I was living out the edict to love thy neighbor, to forgive even when it's hard—especially when it's hard. From that perch, I spent years making sure to humanize those too often considered white trash and racist and redneck, the kind of descriptions too often used to label those who voted for Donald Trump. God, I was convinced, wanted me in that church to tell that story, to explain why even those who loved the Confederate flag were more than their worst moments. I was there to tell the world that they weren't the two-dimensional monsters some perceived them to be. I prided myself on my ability to do just that.

Trayvon Martin's death, or more precisely the reaction to it, convinced me that I should have spent more time doing that for my own brothers. And for the rest of my family.

That's why I'm writing this book. Because my big black family is a beautiful black family, even with all the years some of us have spent behind bars and others spent visiting them there, and even though none of us are quite sure what to do with the shame that comes with being so closely associated with America's prison industrial complex.

I'm writing because I know that my brothers, those who've done awful things for which they were rightly convicted, are not monsters. I'm writing because I know that though I haven't done the monstrous things they have, I'm not that different. In so many ways, it was luck and unearned grace—not solely the dint of my character or solid decision-making or a willingness to work hard—that kept me on the right side of cold steel prison bars.

I have committed arrestable acts; I've just been fortunate to never have been arrested, a reality shared by many, if not most, who dare read these words.

I'm writing because more Americans need to know that complex truth. Without that knowledge, efforts to make our criminal justice system more just and to keep the collective fight against ugly racial stereotypes urgent will continue to wax and wane. Racial progress will forever be at the mercy of the crime rate and state budgets and white fear and black shame. It's why so many Americans could vote for the nation's first black president before supporting a man who rose to national political prominence because of his open bigotry four years later.

None of us is all good, nor all bad. Historians have spent most of this country's history walking that tightrope when dealing with the complexity of our Founding Fathers, powerful, wealthy men who benefited from—and participated in—one of the world's great evils, a system that meant the routine rape of black women and the beating of black men. Still, when we think of George Washington, we think of the cherry tree he never chopped down and the courage he showed by relinquishing the presidency. It has mattered less to us that Thomas Jefferson began raping a young slave girl when she was a teenager than that he wrote that "all men are created equal." We have no problem naming statues and monuments and high schools and colleges in their honor even as many Americans casually express outrage at attempts to humanize the likes of Trayvon Martin and Michael Brown.

Since the 2016 presidential election cycle, the media, in markets large and small, have used barrels of ink and countless minutes on air fleshing out the full humanity of downtrodden white Americans who voted for Donald Trump while relegating the racial ugliness they express to secondary status to the economic and health struggles they face. The message has been clear, that all those white people, from Washington and Jefferson to the Confederate flag–waving white Trump voter in Kentucky afraid the Affordable Care Act might be repealed, are more than their worst moments, their most harmful acts.

Why are so few of us willing to do the same for my brothers and other young black men like them? I'm writing to remind you—to remind myself—that we should.

Growing Up in St. Stephen

> It is easier to build strong children than rebuild broken men.
>
> —Frederick Douglass

Somehow, they made their way out of the bedroom and into the kitchen. I can't remember if Mama was running and Daddy was chasing or if she had simply walked to where the greenish gas stove stood and he followed a few seconds or minutes later. There is no aroma of sausage and eggs and grits wafting through the air in my memory. It looks like the dark of morning, though everyone is fully dressed. The house is serene, eerily quiet.

Then it unfolded as it often did.

I remember seeing him hit her, hearing fist bouncing off flesh, maybe the most god-awful sound the ears of a six-year-old can imagine, especially when it is his father beating his mother.

Daddy was screaming and Mama was hollering and I was cowering in a corner. It felt as though time stood still. Moochie's sudden arrival shook me from my stupor. He was running into the kitchen, grabbing Daddy around the torso, yelling at Daddy, telling Daddy to stop, pulling on Daddy as Daddy kept trying to get back to beating Mama, stopping Daddy's arms from flailing toward Mama and whisking him down the hall and out of view, maybe out of the house. By that point in my life, Moochie had become the man in the family, at least to me. He was physically able to handle Daddy. He was the football player. Moochie was taller and stronger and more muscular and needed every ounce of his strength to get that skinny man away from Mama.

Before Moochie ran into the kitchen, it felt as though the beating would last forever, that my feet would grow roots in the floor as I stared from the corner. But it was over in a flash, because of Moochie. It wasn't the first time my oldest brother saved my mother from my father, nor was it the last time she needed saving from him, or me from that corner.

I can't remember what Mama did afterwards, if she just stood there, grateful she had survived another assault, if she ran sobbing out of the house, pulled me close to her, telling me everything would be all right, trying to convince me as much as herself, or if she even noticed that I had witnessed the whole thing. It's hard to recall those moments perfectly. There are dark, blank spaces in my memory where clear images once resided. I still remember feeling like a coward, that I had let my mother down, that I should have been brave enough to have taken my six-year-old arms and legs and pummeled Daddy, at least long enough to let Mama get away. Instead, I hid, not strong enough to cry, or dry heave, or let out a loud "Stop!" I couldn't talk. I couldn't do anything. I didn't do anything.

Maybe that's why I've spent so much of my life hating the father who helped create me and kept me fed and a roof over my head. I hated him because he beat my mother, hated him because he beat me and my brothers, hated him because he scared me, made me feel small, because I thought he hated me, too.

I hated his leathery brown skin, which matched the color and texture of the belt he used to whip us, as though it was an extension of the fingers he never used to caress us. I hated the way he talked, a gravelly voice only a mother could love, hated the unbalanced gait in his walk that carried his small, sturdy frame from the truck he drove to work to the bedroom he never seemed to leave once he got home, except when he was drunk and the beatings commenced.

I hated Daddy. Maybe that's why I loved Moochie so much. He was everything Daddy wasn't. He smiled. A lot. He joked with us and played with us and protected us, not only from the boogeyman in our own home, but from the bullies down the street. He cared about our spelling bee trophies; I'm not sure Daddy could read or write or spell many words at all.

Moochie led us up and down the back roads of tiny St. Stephen on jogs and marches as though we were in the military. No matter how far or fast he forced us to go, no matter how hot the Southern sun hovering over cloudless skies grew, no matter the sweat-drenched shirts, we loved every second.

"Moochie was like a god to me," my second-oldest brother, Doug, said.

We marveled at his exploits on the football field and basketball court and eagerly awaited any moment he'd teach us how to do it, too. We wouldn't have traded him for Michael Jackson. Besides, he said he'd turn us into the next Jackson 5 anyway, though it was just a pipe dream, given that none of us could carry a tune. Even that didn't matter, because if Moochie said it, we had no choice but to believe it was possible.

He showed up at our school peering into our classes to monitor us. He drove us speeding down the road to visit his girlfriend, laughingly, using only his knees to steer the car down the road. He was the biggest and the baddest on the block, in the neighborhood, in town. He could bully bullies, and would, to make us feel safe. It mattered little that we lived in a poverty-stricken house in a poverty-stricken town among poverty-stricken families if Moochie was around.

"I told Moochie that he seemed to be a better father than their father," Mama said.

There were signs of another side of him that Mama and my oldest sister, Sherrie, noticed but his young brothers mostly ignored or were shielded from. He'd occasionally get arrested for things like petty theft, crimes that eventually became commonplace and more serious, launching us on a series of visits to places with steel bars that would stretch across decades. Berkeley County jail would give way to state prison after state prison. I'd learn later that Moochie's first foray into crime began when he was a six-year-old. He and an afroed friend stole balloons from the five-and-dime.

"It got so bad, we would visit Moochie in jail, and he would be in the same cell with Uncle Harry," Doug said. Uncle Harry, one of my mother's brothers, was a public alcoholic with a mental illness and other health problems.

Moochie would leave the house and not return for days. Mama would stop letting him borrow the car. He would get rides from friends. Mama tried to get help, asked a few counselors to evaluate him. They all said he was too well spoken, too well groomed, too smart, to have any serious issues. He was a young, energetic man, she was told. Moochie's rebellious phase would pass and he'd go on to use his well-developed intellect and craft a successful life and make her proud, they assured Mama.

While those trained professionals were declaring him mentally healthy and stable, Moochie had begun mugging women, "sometimes for fun, sometimes for money."

Mama beamed when Moochie enlisted in the U.S. Army. It lifted a burden, gave her hope that maybe the counselors were right, that her oldest son was maturing, on the road to the kind of life she almost believed he could lead. A year and a day later, he was right back in St. Stephen. He had not adjusted well to military life. He hit a fellow soldier in the back of the head with a pipe as retaliation for a fight that white soldier caused while drunk, a fight that forced Moochie's superiors to put a black mark on Moochie's military record.

"You want to leave now, or you think you can straighten up?" they asked him.

Moochie asked for his release and was granted an honorable discharge, a decision he regrets.

"Man, if I knew then what I know now, I would have stayed in the military," he told me recently. "Man, I would have been able to retire by now, had benefits. Man."

When he got to a small college in Columbia after leaving the military, he almost killed a fellow black student by hitting him in the back of the head with a large stick after that student failed to return five dollars he had borrowed. Prosecutors considered serious charges against Moochie that could have sent him to prison for a few years but decided against it.

"He was different when he came back from the army," Mama said. "The bad headaches that boy would have. He had some problems with his nerves and depression. He was just beaten down in the service. Some days on the base he couldn't perform, then they sent him out on a discharge. They shouldn't have done that. I told Moochie to stay in service longer. He would just lie down and those headaches would be unbearable...and they just let him out of the service. I knew something was wrong. He was trained to shoot and kill."

The long runs Moochie led us on? The ones we enjoyed so much because we got to be in his presence and command his attention? Mama had been forcing him to do those. We hadn't known that our hero would have rather been stealing women's purses and other unsavory things than hanging out with his little brothers.

And he dabbled in drugs. I remember seeing a bag full of colorful pills in his room and was later told it included "speed," or PCP. He was secretly growing marijuana. One day, we were listening to music, goofing around like boys do, dancing and jumping around for no reason. Moochie kept throwing fertilizer over his head and across a fence that separated our yard from another small lot.

"Moochie, what are you doing?" Doug asked him before climbing over the fence and inspecting the plants himself. "That's marijuana!"

"Shhh!! Man," Moochie responded before letting out his signature laugh. "Don't you say nothing, and you better not touch weed until you are at least eighteen. Boy, you smarter than I thought you were."

We didn't fully understand the menace Moochie had been becoming outside of the walls of our small trailer home; neither did we fully appreciate what had happened to Moochie before he reached his early twenties, or the long tentacles of its aftermath. By then, there was Sherrie and Doug, then Willie, then me, Josh, Melody, Jody, a toddling Zadoc, and James, who was still developing in Mama's womb. By the age of fifteen, Moochie had secured his youth driver's license—mature enough to drive supervised by an adult driver, not enough to drive alone at night—and had become a father to a boy, Albert "Smooch" Harris. Smooch was raised among us. Mama was a stabilizing force for our extended family and took in the children of her siblings who died young or had struggles of their own. Not many of us batted an eye when Smooch joined the brood, given his parents' young ages. He was one of us.

Sherrie was closest in age to Moochie but had a more pleasant time with Daddy. She could make Daddy melt like most little girls soften their daddies. She remembers playing with him and getting him to smile and joking with him, sides of him I didn't know existed until she told me about them when I was in my thirties and had a daughter of my own who was doing the same to me.

She would sit in his lap and beg him every weekend to give her the $1.50 she needed to go to the movie theater downtown. Every time, he'd lecture her for fifteen minutes, declare he had no money after working long hours all week to keep the lights on—before giving her just what she asked for, sometimes more.

"He was a traditional father," Sherrie said. "He just worked hard, all the time, and brought every dime home."

She also knew the danger Daddy posed. Sherrie often begged Mama not to go into the bedroom with Daddy, not wanting to hear the sound we all began fearing most, fist on flesh, only muffled by the thickness of the bedroom door.

Moochie, the oldest boy, was the first among us who had to endure the reality that his mother was being beaten routinely, knowing he was powerless to do anything about it. One day he grabbed a kitchen knife. It was a Friday, one of Daddy's drunk days.

"Mama, if Daddy comes back here tonight and bothers you, I'm gonna kill him," Moochie said, tears running down his cheeks.

Moochie hadn't been on Earth for a decade when he stood silently in a corner of the apartment, knife behind his back, waiting for Daddy to get home. As usual, Daddy came home drunk and belligerent. Mama deftly whisked him away from where Moochie was standing.

"I couldn't let Moochie kill his daddy. And I couldn't let his daddy know what was going on," Mama said. "I played it down. I don't know how."

She later told Daddy that things had gotten out of hand, that change needed to come, that pending tragedy hung in the air.

"Herb, you need to be careful; these chur'n are growing up and they are not going to put up with that anymore," she told Daddy.

That warning only seemed to further ignite my father's rage. As Moochie got older and stronger, the beatings that had been mostly reserved for my mother were extended to him.

"Every time he started with me, he would be sure to tackle Moochie first," Mama said.

Days after my mother gave birth for the third time, my father beat ten-year-old Moochie and kicked him out of the house. He was shirtless and barefoot. He ran a couple of miles through a few inches of snow and ice to my grandmother's house. He had to run a lot, until his legs and arms were strong enough to allow him to stand his ground against Daddy.

I experienced the poverty and the domestic violence, as did most of my older siblings. None of us had it like Moochie. He got the worst of it, and longer than the rest of us. He was the first of us to walk through that minefield, which was still lethal when we came along, though was losing some of its explosiveness every year because my parents were aging—and because we had a hero big brother we could rely upon. Moochie never had that luxury.

Fifteen years before becoming an unprepared, clueless teenage father, Moochie was the only one of us born to an unprepared, clueless married teenage girl, a journey that began in a fashion many associate with devoutly Muslim countries, not an American South populated by poor black families.

One day in the mid-1950s, as the Civil Rights Movement was beginning to gain steam, Mama was whisked out of Sunday school and eventually taken a county over to marry a man who was as old as her father. She was thirteen years old. We think Daddy was thirty-nine. Some records show him being born in 1916, though his gravestone says 1933. I've found at least two birth dates for him. The 1916 entry matches up best with family lore. Either way, when Mama was the age my daughter, Lyric, is today, she was forced to marry a man who was somewhere between one and two and a half decades her elder.

Daddy was born either before or during the Great Depression, no doubt subject to the daily horrors and commonplace slights black men and women of his age in the South endured. I know more about the de facto slavery black men my father's age in the South faced than I know about Daddy's actual early life. I don't know if it was happy, or sad, if he grew up in a stable household or was shuttled around from place to place because he was an only child whose mother died during childbirth. I know we are somehow related to the Baileys in Charleston, that we are the direct descendants of slaves and grew up in the only state in the union where more than half of white households "owned" at least one enslaved African. I know Daddy, like my aunts and uncles, was subject to the worst excesses of Jim Crow, his dark skin his primary liability, the illiteracy forced upon him because of that skin color a close second.

Even given that reality, Daddy was one of the lucky black men, not one of the thousands lynched during that period, nor one of the few hundred thousand caught up in an ugly, racist Jim Crow criminal justice system documented by former *Wall Street Journal* reporter Douglas A. Blackmon in *Slavery by Another Name.*

"By 1900, the South's judicial system had been wholly reconfigured to make one of its primary purposes the coercion of African Americans to comply with the social customs and labor demands of whites," Blackmon wrote. "Revenues from the new slavery poured the equivalent of tens of millions of dollars into the treasuries of Alabama, Mississippi, Louisiana, Georgia, Florida, Texas, North Carolina and South Carolina—where more than 75 percent of the black population in the United States then lived."

The South into which my father was born had enacted laws specifically designed to capture black men to be used like cattle by corporations. A black man caught spitting on the street or looking at a white woman led to show trials before KKK-sympathizing judges who benefited from the largesse of stolen black labor. Sometimes those black men were relegated to all-black chain gangs. Sometimes they were literally worked to death. It went on during the period in which a man named Adolf Hitler was enacting similar horrors, and worse, an ocean away.

"Company guards were empowered to chain prisoners, shoot those attempting to flee, torture any who wouldn't submit, and whip the disobedient—naked or clothed—almost without limit," Blackmon found. "Over eight decades, almost never were there penalties to any acquirer of these slaves for their mistreatment or deaths."

This went on as black men and women, and those who sympathized with them, were routinely lynched or bombarded by would-be lynchers. Black bodies dangling from the ends of ropes and burned alive and genitals cut off and stuffed in their mouths wasn't uncommon in the South into which Daddy was born. Men and women like him endured an everyday terrorism that might make ISIS blush. It was so real, so tangible, millions of black people left the South like refugees in their own country. Those who stayed had to always be on guard about their behavior, and that of their children, in the presence of white people. A bitter irony is that white Southerners who daily terrorized black people passed laws to keep black people from fleeing the region, primarily because those black people were critical cogs in the Southern economy. But black people left anyway, often under cover of night, because they believed better economic fates for their families could be had elsewhere.

I hated my father for so long I never gave a second thought to how growing up in such circumstances shaped who he was and why he did what he did to us. I ignored Mama when she said, "Your daddy was a complicated man." Moochie also spoke of Daddy's sins in the context of what black men of Daddy's generation faced in the South.

Daddy hurt us. Good men don't beat women. They protect their children, not force them to seek comfort in dark corners. I didn't need a history lesson to understand that. I didn't want one. I didn't realize the seeds that would blossom into my personal fear of black men—associating violence with dark skin and deep voices—were being planted in those days. Black men were violent and dangerous because my black father was violent and dangerous.

Nothing had changed my mind about Daddy by the time Sherrie picked me up from school early in my sixth-grade year at St. Stephen Middle, a little more than a month before my twelfth birthday. She was subdued as she walked me from the front office to our wood-paneled brown station wagon, the kind made famous by *National Lampoon's Vacation*, gently rubbing on my backpack. That wasn't typical Sherrie.

"Daddy died this morning," she told me softly before starting the car. "We are getting everything ready for the funeral now. If you want to talk about it, we can."

I didn't. I didn't want to talk, didn't need to cry. Sherrie could have told me a thirteenth cousin on Mama's side of the family had died and it would have hit me as hard as the news that my father had succumbed to heart failure.

Daddy and I had never had a heart-to-heart, not about history, his and the country's, nor about why he beat Mama. Given their age difference, was he treating her the way many black parents treated their children to keep them in line? I learned nothing about his side of the family.

I put on a suit like we were instructed to, my Sunday best. I got in the car with my brothers and sisters, maybe in one of the limos the funeral home used to transport immediate family members. I sat quietly during a sermon and eulogy at the church. Kind words were said about Daddy,

I think, and nothing about his drinking and abuse. I didn't listen to a word of any of it. The stirring voices emanating from the choir stand didn't move me.

I stood when told it was time to stand. I closed my eyes when told it was time to pray, but I refused to pray with the rest of the congregation. Daddy, the wife beater, didn't deserve my prayers. I got up and walked past Daddy's open casket near the entrance of the church when told to do that. I refused to take one last look at him.

At Tri Churches Cemetery, a few miles away and across the railroad tracks, the youngest children were passed from the hands of a black man on one side of Daddy's still uncovered gravesite to the hands of a black man on the other side. It's an old ritual with roots in West Africa and the Gullah tradition—a modified version of the culture slaves brought with them to South Carolina—designed to ensure that the spirit of the deceased adult would not come back to haunt the child. I was too old and too big to participate. I didn't want to anyway.

"From ashes to ashes, from dust to dust," the preacher told us as he sprinkled a handful of dirt on Daddy's casket.

We loaded in the cars and left that cemetery. I never expected to return. We made it home to a still-packed house and probably ate fried chicken and greens and ham and macaroni, the kind of food you would have found at every black Southern funeral in 1984.

What I remember most, though, are two large men, one black, one white, wearing suits that would have fit in well on the set of *Starsky and Hutch*, quietly walking Moochie to a room away from the hubbub, putting

Moochie's hands behind his back, placing handcuffs on Moochie's wrists, walking Moochie to a dark sedan, placing Moochie in the backseat, and driving away. I don't remember seeing Moochie at the church or cemetery. My brother Willie remembers Moochie teaching him a few basketball moves before those two men took Moochie back to prison. It would be the only free air Moochie would breathe for decades.

★ ★ ★

Daddy had lived a couple of years after Mama finally left him. Mama always made us visit his wood house across the railroad tracks. On the outside, Daddy's new house looked like an old barn. Inside, it was stuffed with all manner of trinkets and dusty trunks and large pieces of dusty furniture, clutter everywhere. And so were candy bars, particularly Mallo Cups, chocolate coating over a gooey white center. He loved those things, loved sharing them with us. I hated them, thought they were too sweet, but ate them nonetheless.

He and Mama became friends after he left and Mama married again. To me, he became not more of a father, but akin to an eccentric uncle you found some joy in visiting—there was no more yelling, no more leather belt, no more fist on flesh—but would never want having sole responsibility over your upbringing.

It gave me space to reflect and think back to the night Daddy saved us. We were living in what is now commonly known to be a firetrap, a pre-1976 mobile home, before new building regulations by the Department of Housing and Urban Development forced the structure to meet higher safety standards. Before the new rules, the homes were known to burn more quickly and have twice the fatality rate of more traditional homes. Plenty of little black boys and black girls and white boys and white girls born into families who could afford nothing better had lost their lives in such homes.

South Carolina was the center of the mobile home universe, with a higher concentration of such homes than anywhere else in the United States. Ours was green and white, tin sides, tin roof, flammable insulation, thin walls. We built on a couple of bedrooms, mostly made of particleboard and plywood, and a front porch.

I can't remember how old I was, but I know it was in the dead of winter. A fire was blazing in a wood-burning furnace. We were stacked together in one of the built-on bedrooms, which was stuffed with three sets of bunk beds and a gaggle of young men sleeping in our underwear sometimes bumping into each other as we rolled over as we dreamt, at least when we could manage to doze off. The heater was throwing off so much energy it was easier to sweat than sleep. But we did, in fits and starts, until we were awakened by Daddy.

He was running, this time not to beat Mama, but to get to the green fire hose. One pants leg was on, the other dangling, dragging on the floor. Our room was lit up, bright as day, an orange light I will never forget. The house was on fire. Our room was on fire. We came close to being added to the list of poor Southern kids ushered into the next life that way. By the time we realized a fire was trying to engulf our room, Daddy had reached the hose and was putting it out, the thud of the water on the house drowning out the whistle of the flames, long before firefighters showed up in our yard.

For the longest time, I gave Daddy little credit for such things, never once thanked him for saving us from the fire and from poverty and homelessness. He beat my mama. Period. That made him bad, not good. He kept the lights on and the house warm, only used money out of his paycheck to buy alcohol after the bills were paid, brought me into the world. All I've ever wanted to remember was how I felt cowering in that kitchen corner. That's something I'll never forget, something that drove me—drives me—to treat Tracy with the respect Daddy never afforded Mama. It's what convinced me to rush to the aid of a female friend I thought was being beaten by a boyfriend. I stood on their front porch ready to physically harm him until Tracy dragged me back to our car. Violence against women makes me react like little else. That's why I've struggled to not hate my father, write him off as a monster, while providing no quarter for men who hit women.

That's why I couldn't understand why Moochie never much talked about Daddy beating Mama. He'd rather talk about the Shetland pony Daddy bought Moochie when he was twelve or thirteen years old, or the pigeons and ducks and turkeys and hogs, cows and even two horses, Daddy managed to keep around. Moochie likes to remember the garden Daddy kept and the tomatoes, butter beans, string beans, and corn that helped stave off hunger, not Daddy's belt or fists.

"We used to have some good times," Moochie said. "We had problems and all that. But we also had a good, loving home."

I remember a home in which I was frequently afraid and anguished. Moochie says what we faced was best captured by Nikki Giovanni's "Christmas Laughter."

"My family is very small," the poem begins. *"Eleven of us."*

Daddy was intelligent, Moochie said, and tried to steer us to a good life. That's why he disciplined us. He worked hard, never took a day off even when he was sick.

"He might even smile at you from time to time," Moochie said.

Daddy spent a lot of time in deep thought, alone in the backyard, with legs crossed "to get peace like that," maybe smoking a cigarette or drinking a half pint. Or he'd visit his friend Mr. Hudson, a short man who lived near Allen A.M.E. Church, a man who had lost his legs in an accident with the slow-moving train that often chugged its way through downtown St. Stephen.

"He had pieces of a tire and would use those the way we would use shoes, almost like a boomerang, maybe twelve, fifteen inches long," Moochie said of the man.

Daddy would sit with the man for hours at a time, talking to him, laughing with him, listening to the sounds of Shirley Caesar, Otis Redding, James Brown, maybe a little Mahalia Jackson. His lack of formal education, the one stolen from him and most other black people of his generation by a harsh, segregated South, was at the heart of Daddy's ups and downs, in Moochie's vision of our upbringing.

"He and other black men his age didn't have the words to express themselves," so they sometimes resorted to violence, Moochie said. "You gotta be able to express yourself."

The final time Daddy would see his oldest son, he would be at a loss for words again. And neither his fists nor his leather belt could be deployed to soothe his sense of helplessness.

Murder in Bonneau

Despite what's presented on late-night newsmagazines and by overconfident psychiatrists and behavioral experts, there's no way for family members to spot a potential murderer in their midst, no way to "connect the dots," because the dots look so obviously connectable only after the deed is done. For every person who "showed signs" before committing murder, there are a thousand, maybe a million, who show those same signs yet never plunge a knife into someone's neck or pump them full of hot lead.

It's easy to imagine someone you love cheating on his wife, getting into a fight or drunk or high, shoplifting from Walmart, running out on the bill at a local pizza parlor. Those are correctable, commonplace sins and crimes. Murder is not; it is as final as it is sudden. And it always feels sudden, no matter the length of the disturbing history of the man who murders.

That's why it's nearly impossible to imagine a loved one not only having the capacity to take a life but actually doing so. Even domestic violence is hard to envision before fist connects with flesh for the first time. What's worse, if you turn your loved one in on suspicion that he *might* do something awful, you'll be left wondering if you jumped the gun, if you overreacted and wrecked a life that could have been salvaged because maybe, just maybe, he never would have gotten lost in the darkness.

After the killing, after the funeral and the lowering of the body six feet below, and before, during, and beyond the trial, you still struggle with your thoughts. It's a struggle that never ends. You don't want to believe the man you love is a murderer. That's a reality too tough to bear, no matter the facts staring you in the face.

★ ★ ★

Late on April 27, 1982, I was a nine-year-old boy asleep in a room with a couple of wooden bunk beds, blankets on the floor, and my many brothers, when our lives changed forever. I don't know what I was dreaming, or if I was, when Moochie was said to have been a 6.8-mile drive up Highway 52 in a town called Bonneau killing a man named James Bunch.

Moochie was twenty-two years old. He had become a vital breadwinner, his checks from a short stint in the U.S. Army keeping us afloat. After divorcing my father, Mama was left to raise a houseful of kids while forced into disability after years of domestic violence. Moochie was the one who helped Mama and my oldest sister, Sherrie, keep the lights on and insisted his brothers and sisters wore clean, neat clothes whenever we stepped out into the world.

By the time Moochie showed up back home at about 10:30 that night, Mr. Bunch was already dead, stabbed dozens of times in the back and chest and face. Bunch staggered to a neighbor's. A future mayor of Bonneau, then an emergency responder, was the first to reach him, though long after anything could be done to save him.

It was the kind of thing that didn't happen there. Bonneau residents had spent the previous few weeks publicly arguing about whether they even needed a police department. The debate was sparked in part by residents' anger that their town had become a known speed trap to which they often fell prey. Potential speeding tickets scared them more than the thought of a black man with a knife, which seemed as likely as President Reagan retiring in Bonneau after leaving the White House.

★ ★ ★

"Hey, Doug, or Willie, bring me some clothes," Moochie shouted to two of my brothers from the bathroom where he was hiding.

"Moochie! What you doing in there?" Sherrie asked him.

"Leave me alone," Moochie shouted from behind the closed door, where he changed into jeans and a T-shirt, made his way swiftly out of the house, and, like a cat burglar, disappeared into the dark before Sherrie could figure out what was wrong or where he was going.

A few hours later, after his friend told police he had driven Moochie away from the murder scene, officers had made their way to our house, bathing the dark night in blue, asking for Moochie, asking to search the premises, two or three officers out front, another couple hiding in the backyard, readying themselves as though to corner a rat.

"What's going on, sheriff?" Mama asked.

"I can't tell you now, but if it's true, it's real serious. As soon as you hear from him, you need to give us a call," he said, handing Mama a business card before driving off with the set of blue lights and sirens in tow.

They found Moochie before Mama did. He was interrogated for a couple of hours without a lawyer before an attorney from the public defender's office stepped in and told him not to sign the confession he had written, a portion of which reads:

"The way it happened is this. This was the second time that I had seen Mr. Bunch since Saturday. I had robbed him of [$260]. I went to his house and tried to get him to make a deal. He refused the deal. The thought then came to mind to kidnap him. At that point in time, a struggle ensued. Mr. Bunch refused to be kidnapped. Due to the struggle, I pulled out my knife [brown in color] from my pocket and stabbed Mr. Bunch about the face several times. Mr. Bunch then ran out of the house staggering."

We knew about the written confession and the robbery charge from the previous week. But Moochie kept telling Mama he was innocent. We figured he must have been coerced into that admission of guilt by police officers determined to pin the charge on the first young black dude they could find. A few months later, he pled guilty to the murder. That Mama got word only an hour or so beforehand—in exchange, the prosecutor decided not to pursue the death penalty—and had to beg a neighbor to rush her to the Berkeley County Courthouse only fueled those suspicions.

"Mama, I'm doing this for you and the boys," Moochie told her in the courtroom.

Still, we didn't believe, couldn't believe. Mr. Bunch was dead and someone had murdered him. That was a certainty. We held fast to every bit of uncertainty concerning the nature of the crime and the reason for the crime and the response to the crime like a drowning man desperate for just one more breath.

For much of the intervening quarter of a century, it was an article of faith among me and some of my siblings either that Moochie was entirely innocent, or that he'd killed Mr. Bunch in self-defense, or...something. Rumor and myth took root because we never thought to sit down among ourselves or with counselors and therapists to help guide us through. The truth became whatever our individual young minds could imagine, providing a perverse comfort to some of us, and in others planting dangerous seeds that would later sprout in ways no one anticipated. We didn't know any better, couldn't have. It was the biggest mistake we made, the results of which we've spent decades suffering.

My youngest sister, Melody, heard from God knows who that Mr. Bunch had called Moochie and his friend the most unacceptable of all unacceptable words, *"Nigger!"* Most of us in St. Stephen and Bonneau were poor or from the struggling middle class. Pride was a currency worth its weight in gold. It would have been unimaginable for a young black man not to have responded fiercely to such disrespect, especially when it emanated from the lips of a white man whose only alleged advantage was the color of his skin, not the size of his wallet. A fatal fight followed and Moochie pled guilty to spare his friend. That's what Mel's rumor-inspired young mind came to believe despite there being absolutely no evidence any of that happened.

Willie came to believe Moochie got into a fight with his boss over a paycheck.

"They fought, and he probably stabbed him once with the possibility of someone coming in after Moochie and finishing the job" was what Willie remembered of the circulating rumors. There's absolutely no evidence that happened. Moochie didn't work for Mr. Bunch.

"I went twenty-five years thinking that Moochie went to jail because he got into a fistfight and killed someone with his bare hands," my brother Jody said. "That's what all my friends, classmates, and coworkers think."

There's absolutely no evidence that happened.

There were rumors that Moochie had simply fought off an attempted sexual assault, and an out-of-control rage turned a legitimate act of self-defense into a brutal killing. A couple of my youngest brothers and nephews made space for the possibility that Mr. Bunch's killing was Mafia-related, for which Moochie took the fall to protect his family from worse repercussions. I know it doesn't sound rational—why the Mafia would care about a Southern town so small all its residents could fit comfortably inside a New York hotel ballroom is beyond me—but the irrational thinking that leads a man to prison often spreads to members of his family, who'd rather believe the implausible, even impossible, than cope with the all-too-ugly reality that one of its own committed an unspeakable evil.

Mama couldn't shake her doubts, either, even as Moochie initially blamed her for his predicament. It was her fault he had to grow up in a house warped by domestic violence, her fault that the confession and plea deal came about as they did, her fault that he hadn't been a better man. Mama wanted to know more about the role played by Moochie's friend, the one who took him to Mr. Bunch's place that night, the one whose interrogation by police made Moochie a primary suspect almost immediately.

She wanted to know why he had recanted his innocence and went along with a plea agreement she only got wind of at the last second, and how it was possible for a single man to do so much damage to another man's body. Why did the police come back to our house first thing the following morning still asking about Moochie's whereabouts and permission to look through our clothes basket without telling us Moochie was already in custody, Mama wondered.

"Nobody told me anything," Mama said.

A young black man is accused of killing a white man. The murder is investigated by a gaggle of white Southern police officers, prosecuted by a white solicitor. An unsigned, late-night confession emerges, then a rushed plea agreement. It felt like a bad B-movie. Had Moochie become the latest victim of well-documented racist Southern justice? Or was he a villain who had hate in his heart and a knife in his hand?

Mama had desperately sought help for what she had correctly assessed as Moochie's increasingly disturbing behavior that would require sustained, professional intervention if there was to be any hope of curtailing it effectively. Her first-born committing murder? No, not murder. Anything but murder.

"Mama, I'm going to tell what happened when we get to court. I didn't do it," Moochie told Mama, knowing she was desperate to believe her eldest son.

Mama's doubts fueled mine. I knew she didn't suffer foolishness. She never excused our bad behavior. She would leave any one of us in jail overnight if we got in trouble—even if she had enough money to pay the bond—so the stench of the place would convince us to never want to return. I had seen her be right so many times, even in the face of deep-seated skepticism from others, I knew to never dismiss her instincts lightly.

I knew she was stronger than the rest of us. She survived a childhood shaped by poverty and Jim Crow in the Deep South. She adjusted to a forced marriage as a little girl. She made her way into adulthood with her sanity and faith intact, despite all the times Daddy beat her. She handled a forklift in a wood manufacturing plant full of hardened men. She had found the strength to get off the couch, where she had parked herself in disbelieving silence after Moochie was arrested, to visit the crime scene. She stood on the periphery as law enforcement officials were still canvassing the area, unaware that the mother of their top suspect was watching them work. Despite being unable to utter a word for days, she got dressed in her Sunday best and went to Mr. Bunch's funeral, along with Sherrie, to pay her respects.

"I'm sorry for your loss," she sincerely told them, making sure to shake as many hands as possible as family members and friends of Mr. Bunch poured out of the church.

That's why I knew if Mama doubted the story we had been told that I should, too. Maybe that's why I can't, for the life of me, make my brain *see* the night of the murder again, when Moochie rushed into the house, his clothes drenched in splattered blood, as I was awakened from my sleep. It is as though my mind races back to the place it did when I cowered in the corner of the kitchen as Daddy beat Mama every time I try to access the memory of that night.

Moochie was not found guilty in a court of law after a lengthy, fair trial, where we could have assessed the veracity of the evidence. He pled guilty. It may have spared the victim's family a greater emotional burden and the state and county a few taxpayer dollars. But it robbed my family of a reckoning with truth. It did nothing to answer our questions, only fueled our doubts. It felt like a rush to steal him from us as quickly and clinically as possible and to hurt him and us as much as possible. Research shows that poor black men are among the most likely to plead guilty, whether guilty or innocent. Those who plead guilty, even if they are innocent, are less likely to be exonerated later and more likely to have a harder time trying to reenter the world after serving their prison sentences—because when they confessed, they erased all legal doubt.

"When the judge said 'Life,' I saw something go out of Moochie," Mama said. "A piece of him died. A piece of me died, too."

★ ★ ★

I held out hope that maybe Moochie was innocent well into my thirties. Then I went looking for answers. I told myself I would remove my brother hat and put on my journalistic one, that I'd be okay with whatever I found. I pretended to not care about wanting to prove he really didn't do it. In my most honest, or weak, moments, I imagined bringing the Bailey and Bunch families together in a kind of Hollywood ending—hugs and kisses, shared tears of reconciliation—that would bring relief to my long-suffering mother and begin healing our forever-fractured clan.

I want to tell that story. I can't. The facts won't allow me to. Everywhere I turned, digging through old court documents, sitting down with detectives, speaking to family members who were old enough to process what happened, the truth became clearer, that my hero big brother had, indeed, killed Mr. Bunch.

Sherrie found Moochie's bloody clothes, hidden under our house, after he had been sentenced. Doug remembered Moochie telling us that Moochie had tried to rob Mr. Bunch, got into a tussle, and stabbed him "over and over and over again."

"I remember him saying forty-one times," he said. "Moochie wasn't violent. I know that is weird to say. I don't think he was lucid when he did these things. Some drugs affect you in strange ways. Mom and Dad went through some things that he may have witnessed when he was young, but I'm telling you, Moochie was a well-adjusted, well-loved, personable, smart person. He did a lot of bad things, but he always looked out for his family."

My big brother was a murderer, or at least a man who committed murder. Not even an overactive imagination could keep me from facing that reality any longer. With that, my dream of rushing home to tell Mama I could prove Moochie's innocence, could help him get out of prison like the Innocence Project had been doing, died, with no third-day resurrection.

That revelation came twenty-three years after Daddy died of heart failure, just two years into Moochie's prison sentence. Daddy had not needed to overcome a quarter of a century of contemplation and denial before believing his oldest son had committed murder. Daddy visited Moochie at the Berkeley County jailhouse not too long after Moochie had been arrested for Mr. Bunch's murder. He had been living away from us for at least a year by then.

"'I did all I could do with that boy, all I could do,'" Sherrie remembers Daddy saying as he left the jail, never to visit it or Moochie again. "It was the only time I saw Daddy cry."

★ ★ ★

Lindsey Street, a reporter for the *Berkeley Independent,* the local weekly newspaper whose coverage area included St. Stephen and Bonneau, revisited the issue more than thirty years after the murder. Her findings were similar to mine. Moochie was immediately identified as a suspect, given he was arrested for robbing Mr. Bunch the week before, Street found.

The friend who drove Moochie from St. Stephen to Bonneau thought he was taking Moochie to a girl's house or to pick up drugs. Moochie left the car and entered the Bunch house through a window. He confronted Mr. Bunch, trying to get him to drop the robbery charge. Mr. Bunch said no, a fight ensued, and Moochie began stabbing Mr. Bunch, Street wrote.

"Bunch staggered out of the house and into the yard. A fire started inside Bunch's house. Bailey would tell law enforcement the next day that he lit the fire to erase the stabbing evidence, but his cellmate reported Bailey saying several months later that the fire was an accident of a lamp falling over in the scrap," Street reported.

Mr. Bunch was dead by the time emergency officials got him to Trident Regional Hospital at 11:00 p.m.

A young South Carolina Law Enforcement Division agent, Chad Caldwell, arrived at the scene of the murder.

"It was a brutal crime. Any time anybody gets stabbed, there's a lot of blood, and you know that the victim suffered," Caldwell said. He wrote in his 1982 report of the scene there was "a considerable amount of blood" and it was splattered five feet up on the walls. Bailey was picked up by authorities hours after the incident. Caldwell and a Berkeley County Sheriff's deputy interviewed Bailey. "I could see he had remorse. He did regret doing it."

"With prosecutors seeking the death penalty, Bailey pleaded guilty Jan. 12, 1983," Street wrote. "Judge Lee Chandler sentenced him to life with the possibility of parole."

★ ★ ★

By the time of Street's account, I had spent several years reporting on violence and criminal justice, getting an up-close look at how crime ripped apart families the way it had mine. More importantly, the last bit of doubt I had about Moochie's guilt had already been put to rest, not only by what I had found, but by Moochie himself.

For a quarter of a century, Moochie never opened up about the crime. And there was no sit-down between the Baileys and the Bunches, no contrite Moochie explaining to the family of the man he stabbed to death why and how he did what he did. Our families were forever linked on the night of April 27, 1982, but have been walking divergent paths since.

That happened, in part, because there was no practical way to do it any differently at the time. The justice system has since been experimenting with ways to bring victims and convicts together to provide each a greater level of understanding, maybe even reconciliation. In St. Stephen and Bonneau in 1982, it was more likely that rumors of the Ku Klux Klan retaliating against my family for Moochie's crime would be true, or that a young prosecutor would be eager to send him to death row, than the possibility of the Bunches and the Baileys getting together to mitigate the harm done by Moochie's knife. In those early years, Moochie further complicated things by denying his guilt.

After I had seen a psychiatrist to deal with my PTSD and she recommended I explore the crime in depth, and I had begun sharing our painful family history with readers, I got a call from Moochie. I missed it while bathing my young kids. An automated voice from the S.C. Department of

Corrections imprinted itself on my answering machine. He called back maybe a half hour later.

During the first of two fifteen-minute conservations (South Carolina limited calls from prison to that timeframe), I sat mostly quiet as Moochie asked about family members and told me how he was getting his privileges back eighteen months after being a less than perfect prisoner. The next call was different. His voice dripped with shame as he spoke words that were void of their usual bass and buoyancy, the rare time I had ever heard him sound like a little boy. I couldn't see him but imagined him fidgeting in his seat on the other end of the phone and lowering his volume and cupping his hand over the receiver so those around him couldn't hear what he was saying.

He spoke cautiously, hesitantly, but clearly as I relentlessly asked questions. Too many young black men grow up in poverty and face racism—something I'd heard him preach for years—but that can't be used as an excuse, something he had seldom admitted.

He robbed Mr. Bunch a couple of days before the murder, Moochie told me. A friend whispered in his ear that he needed to "take care of Mr. Bunch" if he didn't want to go back to jail. He had been drinking and drugging and wasn't in his right mind, allowing that simple suggestion to take root. A different friend drove him near Mr. Bunch's store. He got out, ran to the store, killed Mr. Bunch, ran back to the car. He changed clothes at our house and went to Dreamland, a juke joint where locals drank, smoked, and danced, and threw away the knife somewhere along the way. He had no diabolical plan to avoid detection; he was simply reacting to the first thought in his mind.

For so many years, he did not understand why we wanted him to show remorse, to admit what happened. We wanted closure and clarity for our own sanity. We wanted him to help us lay rumors to rest, wanted to be able to grieve. We wanted him to seek forgiveness, if not from the Bunch family and correctional officials, then from God, and himself.

Our denial of Moochie's guilt was built upon gaps in our knowledge of the night Mr. Bunch was killed, his on the truth he knew better than anyone.

"I get it, now," Moochie said of why it was important to fully own up to and face the worst act he had ever committed. "I get it. That's what happens when you grow up."

★ ★ ★

I had already given Mama my assessment of what I found about the murder. I hated that South Carolina had no law that demanded the preservation of evidence in murder cases, hated that the police had convinced Moochie to speak without a lawyer present. I hated that the state's prison system, like that of the country's overall, had grown so large between the time of Mr. Bunch's murder and when I got that phone call from Moochie.

I hated that the system remained unfair and that it had corralled too many young black men who had grown up with poverty and domestic violence, like Moochie, I told Mama.

I hated that I could not tell her the one thing she wanted to hear.

"Mama, he told me he did it," I told her.

She half-heartedly questioned me about the conversation I had with Moochie and again about what I had found after a months-long journalistic search but didn't seem to want to really know more. Tears didn't make their way down our cheeks. Neither of us screamed. We wouldn't talk about it again for years.

Talking, for me, about anything, had long been a struggle before that day. The longer Moochie stayed in prison, the worse that struggle became.

A Smile, a Stutter, a Murder

> One of the hardest things in life is having words in your heart that you can't utter.
>
> —James Earl Jones, actor, stutterer

Like many of my second-grade classmates at St. Stephen Elementary, I often looked out through the classroom windows to watch a school maintenance man we called Smiley. He was usually riding a green John Deere tractor. He was short, middle-aged, pecan-colored. His face was round, body slightly chubby, though solidly built. His usual uniform was overalls soiled by a mixture of sweat, grass stains, and freshly cut grass clippings hanging from his pants legs. Almost daily, students laughed at or rushed to be near him during recess.

"Hi, Smiley," many of us yelled to him. "How are you doing today?"

"Kakakakakakak, hoooooow hoooooooow, hoooo-oooow, kakakakakakak, hooooo, hhoooooo, hoooooooo y'all doooooooo dooooo dooooo dooooooinnng ttt-ttt-ttt-tttoday?" He struggled for several seconds, which felt like several minutes.

He stood before us with a trash bag in one hand, rake in the other, portions of his thick afro pushing out from beneath his dingy, snug green John Deere cap. He began tapping his right foot, up, then down. Up, then down. Up, then down, tightening the grip on that garbage bag with every move.

Through the face contortions, through the speech blocks, through the stuttered repetitions, he smiled. That's why we called him Smiley, because his smile never dropped from his cheeks. Not when riding his green tractor. Not when sitting at the table in the cafeteria eating from a small green tray with six compartments, none larger than the palm of his hand, filled with greens and mashed potatoes and gravy and a tiny carton of milk, his knees bumping against the underside of a table only grade-schoolers could find comfortable.

His smile stood steadfast when approached by perky teachers patting him on the back, assuring Smiley his work of mowing the lawn and taking out the trash was being handled superbly. Never did it leave him, never considered leaving him, not when we made fun of the noises struggling their way from his throat through his vocal cords, over his tongue, past his teeth, breaking through his lips and out of his mouth.

His wasn't a beautiful smile. It hung awkwardly from his face, slanting almost, as he tilted his head to the right while his eyelids flapped like a hummingbird's wings. By the time I met him, I was well on my way to becoming a shorter version of him. I was just too busy joining my friends teasing him about the way he spoke to notice.

★ ★ ★

My family members thought stuttering was a nervous condition, the result of emotional trauma or simply evidence that I didn't gather my thoughts well before opening my mouth, or speaking too fast. A young boy losing his hero older brother seemed to be a powerful trigger. That didn't stop the laughter, the ridicule, the "Issac is too dumb to talk" rants from friends and strangers, and couldn't prevent each taunt from silently slicing up my soul. My speech deteriorated into such garble by late in my third-grade year, I was ordered to see a school speech therapist a few times every week.

When I struggled to speak, too many listeners offered advice—slow down, calm down—when their ears would have been sufficient. I tried everything, even rocking the words out of my mouth with my legs and feet the way Smiley had. I began silently counting to ten before every speaking attempt. Each new way worked. For three days or so.

Then more attempts, such as tapping the side of my forehead with my index finger seven times, whispering out the first few words, closing my eyes tightly, practicing the sentences before saying them, slowing down, speeding up, talking with a whisper, sometimes with a shout. You name it, I tried it, and they all worked, for a few days, a few times. Then they wouldn't. I never knew why what sometimes helped me force words from my mouth no longer would. Because of all the laughter, ridicule, and scrutiny, I resented Mama's insistence that I have formal therapy sessions. Her attempts to get professional help to keep Moochie out of prison had not worked. I thought nothing and no one could free me from my stutter.

Ms. Starks, my therapist for most of my preteen and teen years, would sit across from me in a small room and urge me to practice the techniques. A blank stare and folded arms were my most common answer. And silence. For years, the sessions unfolded that way, as begging God to take away my voice, and absorb the hopelessness that tagged along with the stutter, became my mantra. He didn't oblige.

In my early teens, God showed up, at least I thought, in the form of a preacher who claimed to hold the power that could heal all afflictions. Faith healing, hypnosis, and psychoanalysis are therapies stutterers around the world have tried, receiving only limited or short-term relief. I just wanted it to work.

When the preacher visited White Chapel Holiness in St. Stephen, I stood in a long line of others who wanted relief from money woes, failing health, and bad marriages. He poured olive oil on the tip of his finger and touched my forehead, drawing a cross. He prayed, speaking "in tongues," some supposedly spiritual language that could only be understood by your spirit, and I left the church. Silent. Still a stutterer.

It wasn't until eighth grade that I thought I received a break, that someone understood. I sat in the back corner of my English class, as in most classes, longing for invisibility. Our assignment was to make an impromptu speech. The night before, I cried in anticipation of the impending talk. The teacher, Ms. Clarke, a tall, white, stern but kind gray-haired woman, the stereotypical English-teacher glasses clinging to the edge of her nose, surprised us. After my classmates finished their short presentations, the clamor grew for my turn. She quickly silenced the class.

"Because of Issac's condition, he will never be a public speaker, so we don't have to make things hard on him today," she said, or something to that effect.

An awkward smile was my only way of saying thanks. I was relieved that I wouldn't have to stand up in front of the class and try to get words to flow out of my mouth, knowing I'd fail anyway. For many years afterwards, I believed Ms. Clarke, that I'd never be able to overcome. My fear felt confirmed every time I parted my lips to speak and every time I decided to not even waste my time by trying.

★ ★ ★

It didn't take long for Moochie to pile on. In the years before he went away, he made me feel strong, worthy. In prison, he no longer seemed to understand me. He couldn't hear my cries. He had turned into Mtume Obalaji Mfume, a Rastafarian. His long, flowing, sunburned dreadlocks represented the obvious change, as did the hairballs hanging from his peasy, thin beard. His broad, Crest-white smile remained.

His demeanor had morphed from one of boyish awareness and skepticism to spiritual seeker, to conspiracy theorist, to withdrawn man still desperate to remain an active member of the family. He still wanted to be the family protector. He had a new place in the world, and it wasn't only in South Carolina prisons. He was an African warrior whose verbal dexterity and booming voice had begun to intimidate me and impress others. I no longer knew him, even as I tried to hold on to the man who had once been my savior.

During one of our many trips to visit him in whatever prison he had been moved to, Moochie began noticing me retreat into myself. He didn't like it. It must have been jarring to watch his little brother become lamblike while Moochie was roaring like a lion. It was a dangerous state of being, he thought. In a world in which white people were already too powerful, too outspoken, too in control, the black race couldn't afford the meekness of young black boys who needed to become men to reshape not only their families, but civilization itself, Moochie preached just about every time we saw him.

"Being quiet ain't cute, you know," Moochie yelled at me. It felt as though he had saved up that admonishment for months, if not years, and couldn't hold it in, causing him to momentarily abandon a lesson he was giving the family about *"Afri-ckaan peeeoople."*

"You shouldn't be afraid to express yourself. You need to talk," he scolded, jabbing his finger toward me for emphasis before jabbing it into the table.

"I talk when I got something to say," I immediately responded, not giving the stutter time to stop me. His words had made me so angry, or ashamed, it freed me from stuttering's grip, if only for a few seconds.

"Wow! Wow!" Moochie said while leaning back in his chair, smiling, shocked by the fury of my twelve-year-old voice. "All right then. Okay. You got it."

I had lied to him. I often sat silent when I wanted to speak. Stuttering won often.

★ ★ ★

I was a lot like Moochie. His example, his duality, was becoming my duality. He was compassionate at home, a hell-raiser on the streets. I was meek in our house, a terror among my friends. I looked like him. My family knew me as smart and kind and compassionate, introspective, the way we thought we knew Moochie. Yet, even at a young age, there was an arrogance about me.

Mastering books and sports and writing always came easily. I noticed girls noticing me. I had my hero big brother to protect me and tell me how great I was, which made me feel as though I was better than others, so much better that I began acting out in school. I'd quickly finish my work in class and spend the rest of the time trying to get the attention of female classmates I liked and impressing fellow male classmates. I would literally jump over desks in the middle of class, to the astonishment of my teachers, who didn't know what to do with me. My grades were too high, my record and reputation too good, to want to burden me with suspensions. God-given, unearned talents shielded me from the consequences of my actions.

I know, with more certainty than I'd like to admit, that had something not intervened, I would have likely eventually shared a prison, if not a prison cell, with Moochie. Stuttering, the forever thorn in my flesh, tore me from the path Moochie had blazed.

★ ★ ★

One day, I skipped happily to the store to buy a few treats for Doug. Moochie had already been hauled off to prison, and my speech had for some time deteriorated into garble. The thought of being able to keep the few leftover pennies, dimes, and nickels from the purchase had me giddy. It didn't take much to make me happy before stuttering fully took hold. Hurriedly, I walked back to the park to Doug and a large contingent of neighborhood friends. The park was small and surrounded by a chain-link fence. Tall grass had overtaken the park's baseball field, its infield covered with weeds. An enclosed tennis court, its net drooped from years of misuse and pavement cracking in too many places, was located behind the baseball field and across from the basketball court, which suffered similar scars.

"Did you get it?" Doug asked as I rushed toward him, praying my feet would travel faster than his words.

"Did you get the Juicy Juice?" he asked again.

Only a few hundred feet away, chin buried in chest, eyes scanning the earth below, my hand gripped tight the brown paper bag that contained his goodies.

Hurry, please hurry, the words working their way through my brain again and again, *Please, Ikey, hurry. Not today, not again. Please. Hurry!*

Moving ever closer to my destination, I tried to not notice the crowd of kids and especially Kenny, who a few weeks earlier said I was so dumb I couldn't even "speak right" when I'd disappear from class three times a week for speech therapy. It's my earliest memory of what would become a recurring theme in my life. I can't tell you why, but battling my stutter created a hyper-urgency within me to immediately respond to anyone asking me a question (except my speech therapist) and likely worsened the speaking disorder. Doug wasn't trying to force me to speak in front of everyone, he was simply asking me a question, but it felt like a command nonetheless. I find myself fighting against that instinct in conversations and during interviews three decades after the scene that day in the park.

"Did you get the Juicy Juice?" Doug asked again.

My heart was pounding, demanding freedom from an uncooperative chest. Sweat dripped from my palms. My upper body tightened so rapidly it felt as though a large fist was pushing against me. There was no need to fight against them any longer.

"They didn't have...," I started, my eyes still concentrating on the earth below my feet. "...No Juuuiiiiii."

My feet stopped just a few yards away from Doug as the playground and too many pairs of eyes engulfed me. My legs would move no farther. My brain refused to comprehend, leaving me in a lurch.

"They diiiiii diiiiiii ddddddd dddddddd. Thhhhhhhhhheeeeeeeeeey. Um. Ah. Um. Ah. Um. Ah. Um. Ah. They ddddddddiiiiiiiii dddddiiiiiiiii. Um. Um. Um. Um. Um. Um. Um. Thhhhhhhhhh. Um. Ah. Um. Ah. Um. Ah. Um. Ah. Ah. Ah. Um. Ah. Um. Ah. Um. Um. Um. Um. Um. Thhhhhhh..."

All around became a blur. The loud laughter easily penetrated that veneer. My heart rate sped up uncontrollably beneath my burning chest. My arms no longer felt attached to my body as they went numb. The lips on my face seemed not to be my own.

As I desperately tried to tell my brother the convenience store didn't have his flavor of twenty-five-cent juice, *Please let me, please, just this once, let me talk,* the words trudged their way through my brain, as they had so many times before, but to no avail.

The words, the right words, the ones being sought, those that had flowed swiftly and easily a thousand times through my head, couldn't be accessed. *Please go through my lips, just this once. Please!* But to no avail.

It seemed as if every kid in the park, Kenny and his taunts, Melvin from the other side of the woods, Eric and his smirk, had stopped to watch my mouth perform tricks on me. It didn't matter if they had actually stopped swinging in the swings or twirling on the merry-go-round. To my mind, they had. I was just a little boy whose mouth was amusingly failing him again, this time in front of a hostile crowd.

Moochie wasn't there to scare them off.

It'll be over soon. The next word will be the breakthrough, I silently lied to myself. *It's almost over. They're gonna come out. They have to. I can do this.*

"They diiiiii diiiiiii ddddddd dddddddd.

"Thhhhhhhhhheeeeeeeeeey. Um. Ah. Um. Ah. Um. Ah. Um. Ah.

"They dddddddiiiiiiiii dddddiiiiiiii.

"Um. Um. Um. Um. Um. Um. Um. Thhhhhhhhhh. Um. Ah. Um. Ah.

"Um. Ah. Um. Ah. Ah. Ah. Um. Ah. Um. Ah. Um. Um. Um. Um. Um. Thhhhhhh..."

Then my legs began to move as my body found an alternate route to produce fluent speech, a route that had been working for much of the previous week. My weight shifted to my right leg, which was a step in front of the left. Then it shifted to my left leg, then back to the right. Right leg. Left. Right. Left.

This will work. It has to. It just has to. It's worked before, I pleaded with myself.

The movements resembled those of a little boy atop one of those plastic rocking horses stationed in front of dime stores, only there was no horse, just an attempt by a young frightened stutterer to rock his words, and himself, free. After too many failed attempts, it began working. Words began breaking from stuttering's grip when my front foot hit the ground, the speaking taking the requisite pauses as the weight shifted back to the left.

"Thhhhhhh" became "They didn't have," left foot, "No Juicy Juice," left foot, "In the store." "So, I bought," left foot, "This candy," left foot, "And juice," left foot, "Instead." Those words, too, stumbled from an uneasy mouth.

They were out, allowing peace to join me onstage, where it was, for just a second, easy to pretend nothing else mattered. All around, laughter rained, amazement dripping from every face. I tried to not notice the kids literally rolling on the ground holding their stomachs as they thoroughly enjoyed my performance. I walked past that satisfied audience and out of the park and into my house, feeling defeated. Again. I sought refuge in a locked bathroom.

Kenny was right, I'm too dumb to talk.

I couldn't stop the tears. I made sure no one else knew I had cried them. I didn't leave the bathroom until they dried up and I had wiped my face clean of any residue. It wasn't the first time I comforted myself with aloneness. It wouldn't be the last. It wasn't anger I felt. It was confusion. And fear. I didn't know what awful thing I had done to deserve such an existence.

Those kinds of days sent me searching for answers I wouldn't find for a couple of decades, sent me searching in all the wrong places. They led me to smile more, like Smiley, even as an initial confusion slowly burned its way into a simmering anger. At least people patted Smiley on the back for keeping the schoolyard clean. Maybe one day they'd do the same to me.

Hearing my own voice made me want to vomit. Days like those led me to the back corners of classrooms and to the periphery of conversations, to countless bathrooms, and behind many locked doors. It was hard figuring out who I should hate more, me for being too dumb to talk, or them, all of them, those who laughed and pointed and said nothing and too much and tried to help and inflicted pain and suffering.

Moochie was gone. And I had to get into a station wagon and ride two hours or more just about every weekend to see him in a dark, dank place only to have him chide me about not expressing myself enough, about the need to speak more frequently, more clearly, as though it should be as easy for me as it had become for him. I needed his protection and understanding. I got neither. The last thing I wanted was more lectures from more people telling me all the things they had discovered that would surely free me from my stutter, including the woman from church who told Mama, as I looked on in silence, to put a lizard on my tongue to scare the stutter out of me. Mama declined to take that piece of advice.

I wanted someone to save me; desperately needed someone to save me. Moochie was available neither physically nor emotionally. Mama sent me to speech therapists at school, cobbled up money to get me face-to-face time with private therapists, and prayed for and with me. It didn't work. I still felt alone.

Doug was busy battling a stutter of his own, though it didn't seem to stump him the way mine stumped me. He wasn't one of the kids who simply grew out of a childhood stutter—which is true of most young stutterers—but it always felt as though he could control his better, that it didn't handcuff his emotional life the way mine had. He was also trying to figure out how to operate in a world in which he suddenly became the oldest male in the house before Mama remarried.

Moochie's godlike presence made it difficult for me to appreciate Doug's steadfastness; the psychic scars left by Moochie's absence made it impossible to notice that Doug's example was shaping me as much as Moochie's. My baby picture may more closely resemble Moochie, but the footsteps I followed were more like Doug's. He just got shit done no matter what—whether tearing apart and rebuilding computers and VCRs to make them work better, being unafraid to grab a microphone and stand in the middle of a stage and talk, finding unique non-corporal forms of punishment to help keep his younger brothers in line, or helping his kids blaze their own trails—which is the way family members and friends describe me.

Willie and Sherrie were going through their adjustments as well in our new, strange reality and provided the stabilizing forces I needed but never got from Daddy and was robbed of when Moochie went to prison. That's something else prison did that I'm only now realizing, made me so long for a man behind bars it blinded me to what was staring me in the face, that the three older siblings who remained, Doug, Willie, and Sherrie, were saving me in a way Moochie never did, and couldn't. The path Moochie had taken, for a complex set of internal and external reasons, would have led me to a dark place, too. But my other two big brothers and my older sister, their presence, provided me other examples. They preached and practiced personal responsibility and the value of family and education. Stuttering forced me to see the world differently; they reminded me that good outcomes were still possible despite the obstacles we faced.

It's also truth that there was no one to guide any of us through the most perplexing period of our lives. We all were too busy trying to survive to consider, or even understand, broader, long-term implications. It's likely why decades later we have loving, though not necessarily affectionate relationships like the ones you see in movies between adult brothers and sisters. Through text messages and Facebook posts, we'll send birthday wishes and happy Mother's and Father's Day well-wishes. We try to get together at least once a year to laugh together and gently scold each other and catch up on the latest gossip about St. Stephen, with most such gatherings built around Mama. No one really frets if we don't, though. And when some of us have faced life-altering or life-threatening events, the rest of us have heard about them afterwards, if at all. Prison doesn't only separate you from the loved one convicted of a crime; it can build subtle barriers among family members that are hard to spot and harder to reconcile. The complexity and oddity of stuttering made my journey even more unique and difficult to comprehend. My family didn't understand what I faced; neither did I.

I didn't know if the stutter was God's fault or mine, didn't know what was wrong, only that something was. Didn't know what was broken, and didn't know how it could be fixed, or if it could be fixed, or needed fixing, or hiding from, or confronting, or accepting, or despising.

It was hard to understand, knowing that while days such as the one in the park were always just over the horizon, I could from time to time stand on a real stage in front of hundreds of people to participate in a spelling bee and take home a first- or second-place trophy. Maybe it was the cadence demanded by the bee, where everything was in rhythm, every call by the announcer precisely measured, or maybe it was the endless practice and repetition that freed me in those few hours.

Maybe that's why I cried walking home from school on report card day in the second grade after receiving a C in reading, one of the few scores below an A I'd ever post. My older brothers and sisters laughed at my tears at what seemed like a silly overreaction. But that C cut deep. Moochie's imprisonment meant my family wasn't perfect. The stutter meant I wasn't. My grades, the thing over which I had most control, were supposed to be perfect, to shield me from the shame of stuttering; now they were imperfect, too.

★ ★ ★

Who can't open up their mouth and talk? Who can't, just...talk? I'm tired of doing this, tired of hearing people laugh at me, tired of wondering if and when and where the words will start coming out like my brothers', tired of everything. I wish I didn't ever have to speak again. Life would be better than this. Who can't talk? Nobody, except you, Ikey. That's so stupid. You're so stupid.

Wishing for Tonka trucks and train sets for Christmas turned into wishing, demanding, and praying for speaking fluency. After the day in the park, and so many like it, my eyes often found their way to the earth moving beneath my feet. The bumpy, bubbly dark pavement. The brown soil littered with broken glass. The overgrown grassy fields. The uneven, weed-infested sidewalks. The rough terrain of white-rocked roads.

No longer did looking deeply into the brownness of the eyes of my grade school crushes lift my spirits. I stopped noticing the thickness of anyone's lips or the curves of their foreheads, because as my stuttering became my cage, my eyes began focusing downward. I couldn't look anyone in the eyes while speaking, because it reminded me that people noticed me. I hated even looking at myself when

I was alone. Listening became everything, speaking little more than a bad joke. I didn't appreciate it enough at the time, that while I was coping with a challenging, even ugly, transition in life on this side of those barbed wire fences, Moochie was doing the same from the inside.

Bad White People

I can't remember the day I realized Moochie had grown to hate white people; I know he was a few years into his life sentence. His dreadlocks had already grown long, his thinking a curious mix of conspiracy and inspiration, the conspiracy concerning the sins of white people, the inspiration the nobility and resilience of black people in the face of white supremacy. He had long since begun sounding like a lunatic who had the intellectual capacity and wherewithal to look up from time to time and take in a few gulps of sanity—that's when he would smile and laugh with us, say something silly just because—before diving right back into the crazy. It went on that way for years. Had a fellow inmate told me Moochie howled at the moon every midnight, I would have believed him.

It's exceedingly difficult to convey just how different Moochie had become. Many years later, when we both were men and after the fog had finally begun to lift, he'd tell me even he didn't realize how much prison had transformed him. To try to reach him intellectually was to flirt with an emotional event horizon, your own sanity in jeopardy of being forever lost. It got that bad. His letters were always a good window to his mind.

Here's a taste of one of them:

Now 9-14-381 A.B.A.

Rastafari Greetings!

smile,...

Khafre,...Malkia Tisji,...smile,...

Peace, Uhuru (Freedom) Belongs to you,...smile,...

Heh, Folks, smile, My Beautiful, Strong, Proud,...and indomitable Brother and sister...smile,...Victorious Consciousness,...smile...Thank Jah Jah,...Everything is gonna be alright,...smile,...

Struggle touches and comes to all,...at some point in life. It is good,...and important when one,...when we can look back, reflect,...and see how we got over,...and got thru,...various periods of struggle in our life/lives.—smile—in our personal and individual lives,...and in our lives, as a race, as a people, smile,...

History...know your history and you will always be wise.

Recently,...rather than just sitting around,...and watching,...the occurrences and behaviors that go on,...I decided ad have had to take initiative myself,...in bringing attention to Afrocentricity ad Rastafari,...and Afrocentric-Afrikan-centeres of viewing the world,...our history,...our culture,...our predicament,...and etc. Ah,...I've had to,...thru force. No one else was stepping up and doing it,... intentionally,...consciously,...and on a consistent basis.

For the past 2 days,...what I have done is use a method,...that I employed,...the years,...while at Evans prison on lock-up...i.e.—reading aloud.

And so, presently, I am reading books aloud,...at the

door,...at the cell door,...—Afrocentricity—in particular,... and a few others,...—for the salvation of our sanity,...as Black men,...in an extremely dehumanizing environment, ...such as lock-up,...which is a prison within a prison.

Afrocentricity,...I know,...can save us,...and hold things together in an intelligent manner,...and prepare us for our mission and our lives,...once re-entering the outer society...

Afrocentricity is a weapon,...the use of knowledge, intelligence, our history, our culture,...to defend our minds and guard our sanity...

Afrocentricity does this for Black people,...no matter where Black people are,...no matter what condition/circumstances,...Black people find themselves confronted with.

Thank Jah,...I have tested it,...for years,...and it has always seen me thru...

Consciously, I've been working with Afrocentricity since the late 80's,...or so. Thank Jah for Dr. Molefi Kete Asante...smile,...he is/was the instrument used to pen the book Afrocentricity,...—but really,...Afrocentricity is our history and culture,...created and sustained and passed on by those Black people,...loyal, dedicated,...and committed,...to the salvation,...liberation,...independence,...and self-determination,...and empowerment of our people,... Black people all over the world.

So, O.K.,...again,...I ask/request that you and Malkia Triyi,...get your own copies of Afrocentricity,...read, study, discuss, Afrocentricity,...and its place in your lives, and the lives of our people. Again,...I ask/request that you make sure that each and every household in our family/families,...get and/or have their own copies of Afrocentricity,... and that it is discussed,... read,... utilized,... and tested.

Afrocentricity can hold its own... among and/or against any and all ideologies,... and/or ways,...

Read the book,... and know this... for yourselves,...

Rastafari,... too,... is like that,... smile,...

But,... it seems that it is easier for one to come to a consciousness of Rastafari,... once having understood,... Afrocentricity, yeah, easier...

In prison visiting rooms and on the phone, he spoke the way he wrote. He needed to speak the way the rest of us needed air. Not only the words, but the spacing between the words and the pacing and the unique system of punctuation and spelling—even verbally—and the jumping between thoughts, they first kept us united, because of their strange nature, then they became a barrier—because of their strange nature. We wanted him to be Herbert Lee "Moochie" Bailey Jr. from St. Stephen, the dude with the short afro who played sports, kept us safe, and laughed a lot. During those years, all we ever got was a new man who had taken on a new name, Mtume Obalaji Mfume, and had assigned each of us African-sounding names few of us ever used. He stopped calling me Ikey and crowned me Ras Kharfe. It was the name of an Egyptian king for whom some believe the Great Sphinx was built in about 2500 BC, a religious heretic.

Each of Moochie's letters had the same central theme, the beauty and importance of the black family and how it must fight—and hard and with everything—to not be destroyed. He persisted in the belief that the more we understood that history and embraced it, the better able we'd be to fight off the tentacles of the white rage and sin that had already fractured our family. He'd say it with the urgency of a little boy fleeing his family's burning home in search of a firefighter.

We all had suspicions about white people. Were they trying to cause us harm? Were they trying to take advantage of us? Look down upon us? But we never talked about white people the way Moochie had begun to. Being fueled by an anger against white people can only take you so far. It doesn't mean we forgot present-day or past realities. How could we? We daily walk on ground where enslaved Africans toiled. We live among forests and town squares where black men and women were lynched. We watch our sons handcuffed and beaten and shot far too often by men with badges and batons. We couldn't forget if we wanted to. It's just that we know that anger, though a necessary part of black life that has inspired black progress, will never be enough to help us thrive in an environment in which our skin color forever makes us suspect.

It's one of the peculiar things about being black and growing up in the South. Racism can be embedded in just about everything around you, but you'd lose yourself if you didn't wear a kind of partial racial blindness, letting only a bit of it at a time into your conscious awareness. That's why it's always funny to hear white colleagues, friends, and neighbors declare that "all black people think about is race." They don't know that the racism and discrimination we feel compelled to fight openly is the tip, not the iceberg. In prison, Moochie took off the blinders and let four hundred years of white racial sins overwhelm his senses, blinding him to everything else.

My parents' generation had it particularly difficult, trying to get ahead in a region created to keep them behind. To fight or deflect was a common struggle. They had plenty of reasons to loathe white people, but didn't. Protecting their own sanity was one of the reasons they chose that route. Their Southern Christianity was a primary motivating factor also. Forgiving and praying for those who had done you harm was a pillar of the faith. To survive generations of beatings and rapes and murder, and threats of beatings and rapes and murder, and still be able to see the complex humanity of your oppressors is no small feat. Most Americans are incapable of doing so, which is partly why the prison industrial complex has grown exponentially. Bloodlust, fear, and hatred fueled the unprecedented rise in incarceration as much as a thirst for justice. The people hurt most by the system and the crime are the best-positioned to understand that truth. My parents' generation understood that well.

For our generation where I grew up, there were few direct white-black clashes to witness. The discrimination we faced was mostly systemic—segregated schools, white power structure, uneven policing and sentencing—not visceral. Our minds were more susceptible to abuse than our bodies, though that doesn't mean our bodies were spared. But on occasion, Mama would tell us it was sometimes easier to deal with white people than some black residents, because the relationships would be transactional, clearly defined. Why Moochie needed to adopt a thinking that turned all of that on its head, we didn't know.

"Don't bust his bubble," Mama would warn me.

She was conflicted, knowing she'd never accept the rest of us speaking about white people the way Moochie did. She usually barked out commands to make herself clear about such things. But she only whispered when telling me to be careful about probing Moochie's state of mind. He was in a place where he had to stuff towels under the door to keep large rats out while trying to sleep and had to be on guard against potential physical attacks. That changes a man, she said.

Mama was stumped about how to deal with this new, emerging Moochie. We all were. I just dove in anyway, a journalistic tendency animating me long before I officially became a journalist. I began asking Moochie how he could hate white people, given what he had done.

"It's disrespectful, man," I told him. "I know good white people."

"But you don't know what they *stole* from us!" he returned with an accent that sounded more Jamaican than Southern African-American, as though he had taken on another personality. "You don't know how many of us they killed over all these centuries. Mother Africa. They raped Mother Africa. They raped our women. They abused our children. They did this to us! Everything they've touched, they turned it into evil. Know your history, man! Know your history!"

I told him it was wrong to label all white people that

way, about white friends and families in St. Stephen I admired, that he had once admired. He didn't care.

"*They* raped Mother Africa," he thundered.

I wish I'd had access to the *Saturday Night Live* skit that went viral during the 2016 presidential election cycle to show him then. In it, Tom Hanks played the part of a working-class white Trump supporter participating in a game of *Black Jeopardy*. The black host and contestants grew more astonished at every correct answer Hanks's character got right—something that had never happened with previous white players. The brilliance of the skit (and it was brilliant) wasn't that it was belly-aching funny, though it was; it was that it perfectly illustrated, in an *SNL*-exaggerated way, the values and life outlooks shared among black and white people of a certain culture. It even touched on the racial land mines that keep the two sides from more frequently embracing those similarities or building black-white coalitions.

Blacks and whites in the working class, particularly in the South, have had similar struggles and found exhilaration in many of the same things. But findings from groups and studies such as the Equity and Excellence Commission, the National Child Abuse and Neglect Data System, *Social Policy Report*, and the Campaign for the Fair Sentencing of Youth have shown that a higher percentage of black kids were (and are) concentrated in crappy schools and subject to harsher forms of discipline at home, in the principal's office, after Sunday school, and in the courtroom. That does not mean a significant percentage of the white working poor hasn't suffered from those things, because they did, and do. It's possible to acknowledge that black people had it worse but that many white people faced daunting struggles and unfairness, too.

My stepfather was a stock car driver. Fishing and deer hunting and four-wheelers and dirt bikes and dirty T-shirts were common among blacks and whites in our region. Together, we enjoyed TV shows—*The Dukes of Hazzard,* with an orange car emblazoned with the Confederate flag as the star, most prominent among them—PhD candidates in sociology dissect today as racially demeaning to black people. You want good fried chicken, watermelon, sweet tea, or shrimp and grits and boiled peanuts? Black and white families throughout the South could show you the ropes. Paula Deen, a white woman, is one of the South's best-known cooks, yet her style can be found in numerous black kitchens in the region.

Boy did we love Ric Flair, the long-haired blond wrestler, almost as much as we loved white Jesus with his long hair and blue eyes and beard. You'll find his white face (Jesus's, not Flair's) hanging on the walls of plenty of white homes and churches throughout the South—and black ones. If you really want to understand the allure of energetic black preaching, don't visit Bishop T. D. Jakes at the Potter's House in Dallas today; pop in a VHS of Jimmy Swaggart, the white, charismatic TV evangelist who began his career preaching from the back of a flatbed trailer.

That's the messy truth of race in the South. Even as the dogs and water hoses and hangman's nooses and discriminatory laws were used to hold back black people, there was always enough misery—and hope and blind faith in

God, country, and gun—to go around. It's hard to have been black and lived in our part of the South and not have had to process a nasty word from a potbellied, tobacco juice–spewing, overalls-wearing old Southern white man and then later come across a white man who looked just like the first who pulled up next to you, helped you change the flat tire on your car, and handed you a few watermelons and ears of corn to take to your mama.

It's true that black women were often relegated to jobs cleaning up after white people; that was true for Mama and Aunt Doretha Reid, one of my mother's younger sisters and my last living aunt, even after she left the South for New York. It's true that white men in unions practiced a demeaning form of Jim Crow, reserving the best factory jobs for themselves, even when they were illiterate and had to get educated black workers, who were paid less, to read safety manuals for them on the floor of steel mills and other factories, where dangers abounded and limbs and fingers were not infrequently severed. (It was worse for black women, who were treated harshly by white and black men who felt their jobs were being threatened by the presence of the other gender.)

Moochie had long left behind the teachings of White Chapel Holiness Church, where a couple of generations of our family worshipped, and replaced it with Rastafarianism. He didn't notice the irony. He was preaching a version of what the Christian faith had taught us, that one day there would be a reckoning, that nobody knew the day nor the hour, even though it was close at hand and signs had already begun revealing themselves.

The evangelical movie *The Burning Hell* was screened in our church when I was young. It was crude, bloody, violent, and a must-watch, even for kids, because it supposedly illustrated what happened to those who refused to embrace Christianity. I could barely sleep and was deathly afraid of making a mistake for about two weeks after seeing it. I watched it again decades later to see if it would have the same effect. It didn't. It was clear, though, that had Prison Moochie the ability, he would have produced a movie just like it, only with black people as the protagonists.

At that time, Moochie believed white people had been put on Earth to commit evil. That's why they had owned slaves. That's why they carried rifles and road horseback and lorded over black prisoners as those prisoners were forced to do backbreaking work in miles-long fields, for pennies on the hour. White people built those prisons where he had been housed. White people set the rules for when black men inside those walls could go to sleep and wake and eat and shit and shower. It didn't matter if the guards were black like him or that a significant minority of his fellow prisoners were white. It only mattered that they all were there on orders given from white wardens, orders handed down by white governors and white senators and representatives and presidents who wouldn't mind seeing black people disappear if their labor and bodies weren't useful tools for the perpetuation of white supremacy and commerce.

Everything he said was simultaneously grounded in a world of his own creation and the very real history of the

United States of America. Racial injustice was real. It was a foundational reality of this country when the original thirteen colonies stood together and fought off a menace based an ocean away—yelling give me liberty or give me death, writing that all men are created equal—to establish a democracy that remains well into the twenty-first century. White people have systematically harmed and exploited black people. It's not happenstance that black men have always been overrepresented in the prison system, even though the history of white men raping and rioting and plundering is much more pronounced than black criminality. It's not just a coincidence that black men face longer sentences and a higher conviction rate than similarly situated white men and are on the wrong side of racial disparities at every level of the criminal justice system and beyond. All the while, the cops, who are considered by a significant number of black people as pawns to keep black men in their place rather than to protect and serve, have seen their approval among white people in Gallup rankings rise to all-time highs, no matter how many times they shoot a black man in the back as he runs away or sever a black man's spine while he's in custody or shove a broken broomstick up his rectum.

Unrelenting racial barriers constructed by law and custom could never extinguish people's ability to find ways to embrace beyond skin color differences. Though almost all the people in the region were white and black, the everyday reality of race relations never was. In the American South, despite all the tumult, and sometimes because of it, a common humanity always found a way to show itself in everyday interactions between black and white.

Moochie knew that—because he had lived through it longer than I had. Prison Moochie stopped believing. He had no patience for stories about "good" white people because, in his new view of the world, no such creature had ever walked the Earth. Black people needed to face that reality and act accordingly, especially people like his stuttering little brother.

Those humane, everyday interactions between black people and white people occurred when my daddy was born during an era in which hundreds of thousands of black men were stolen from the streets and their families, convicted on bogus charges and sold to a variety of U.S.-based companies who worked them nearly to death. It was happening when my brother was born a half decade before the Civil Rights Act. It was happening when I was born four years after black people were finally able to fully exercise their right to vote. It was happening when my son was born in the shadow of the 9/11 attacks. That reality remains true today and was true when Moochie wrote cryptic letters and when we sat across the table from each other inside prison visiting rooms.

Prison Moochie didn't do racial nuance.

From one of his letters:

O.K.,...the next thing,...the diet.—Whoa! Now that is all important! Whoa! Smile,...Ask me,...I know,...smile,... But,...Heh,...O.K., for years,...I been stop eating meat,... smile,...But, even that is not enough. No. No. No.—Brother,... because of conditions,...it is now necessary to really,...take control of diet. The Honorable Elijah Muhammad counseled

1 meal per day,...or 1 meal every 3 days,...—yeah,...serious...I myself still struggle with breads...

Look into this for yourself,...and counsel each and every family household and member,...to seriously consider and try this for themselves. The less one eats,...the more work one can get done,...—O.K.,...and of course, Rasta say No meat, no animal flesh, no animal product...and no bread made from white flour,...nor cakes,...That stuff puffs one up,...and clogs up one's digestive system. Of course,...this is a very disciplined way to view and deal with one's diet. It is also, the most intelligent, in terms of health consciousness and quality and longevity in life.

O.K.,...and this is especially important for Black people,...especially in light of the pressures that Black people face constantly, from day to day...—as Black people confront, white racism,...injustice,...exploitation,...and the constant bombardment of anti-Afrikan rhetoric and symbols.

O.K.,...warriors,...you know,...

From another:

O.K., my views...that is,...the Black Political Prisoner and Prisoner of war,...perspective on prisons,...the Justice System, and this country.—Bro,...here's a few key terms,... names,...and books to research and familiarize yourself with,... and to help shed light on your book.—The number one book—you already know..."Afrocentricity,"...—O.K.,...know/study/research the books and lives of,...Assata Shakur,... George L. Jackson,...Malcolm

X.,...and above all,...Mumia Abu-Jamal, (who is framed and presently on death-row,...in Pennsylvania,...) and the MOVE prisoners,...and the over-all situation of Blacks and Prisons in this Kountry. It is mentacide and genocide. It is war—read,..."Schooling the Generations In the Politics of Prisons" by Chinosole. Yeah, man, there's tons of connections,...and pieces necessary to bring consciousness. My story is simply a part of the larger story.—The Black Panthers,...The Nation of Islam, especially, during the 60's,...and Cointelpro.

"What about a five-year-old white boy?" I kept pushing Moochie. "Why is he a threat?"

I wanted to pin him down rhetorically. There are sets of circumstances that lead people to do awful things, I argued. If we recognized those circumstances sooner, maybe we could head off the awful act before it manifested itself. Doing bad is neither inevitable nor inherent, I tried to desperately convince him, or myself.

"What about a five-year-old white boy?" I asked him again. "Why should I hate him?"

Prison Moochie answered without hesitation.

"Because he grows up."

★ ★ ★

Moochie had been in prison less than a decade when a little white boy forever altered my view of the world. He was a member of the KKK, the infamous domestic terror group known for its history of lynching black people, the group we initially feared in 1982 was still strong and prominent enough to do us harm in retaliation for what Moochie had done.

That little white boy may have been ten years old when our paths crossed. He was leaning against a small pole next to a makeshift stage from which his older family members, dressed in iconic KKK garb, yelled through bullhorns and microphones about the nastiness of black people and the importance of maintaining white power and purity. I was a rising high school senior and had just attended a church service with my future wife in the Charleston church where a quarter of a century later a young white supremacist named Dylann Roof would make international headlines by killing nine black people during Bible study to start a race war.

I rushed from church, eager to join in the hatred for the KKK shared by what seemed like thousands of other people, black and white. We gathered in the summer heat in the shadow of a three-story-tall monument built in honor of one of the nation's most prominent slavery proponents in the heart of the city where the South fired the first shots to begin a Civil War. Amid all that noise, all that chaos, controlled by black and white police officers in riot gear and on foot and horseback, my eyes were drawn to that little boy. His body language told me he didn't want to be there, or maybe that's what I hoped his body language was saying. He did not wear a smile. He was not yelling "white power" or "niggers go home." He was silent. A look of fright and confusion emanated from his reddened cheeks.

Did he hate his family for forcing him into the middle of something he could not have understood? Did he hate the crowd for hating his family? Maybe he had created a fictional place in his mind the way Moochie had done to psychically escape prison. Moochie's dreamland was of African kings and queens. Maybe that little white boy's was of that big park emptied of those loud adults and instead full of kids playing tackle football and tag and running and climbing trees.

Nearly two decades later when I began writing a weekly column about race relations, I featured him. It was jolting to readers that a black man who had grown up in the South had chosen to empathize with a young Klan member. I wanted to unsettle them; it's often the only way to get people to see the messiness of race anew. It worked. While Moochie was behind bars telling everyone about the need to adopt a black-centered worldview, I was being thanked by white readers for forcing them to face the issue of race in a way they could handle.

On the day of the march, I couldn't stop looking at that little white boy because he wasn't what I expected the KKK to be. They were supposed to be ten feet tall, men who could steal your body and demoralize your spirit. Instead, they were a couple dozen poor white people who yelled bad words through bad teeth and wore tattered clothes. I began feeling sorry for the people I had been sure I needed to hate. I didn't want to empathize with them and tried to force myself to forget that they were simply trying to navigate a too-often unkind world. I didn't want to see them as humans, only as monsters.

That's when I realized some of what Moochie had been preaching had been affecting me. Even as I was pushing hard against the white hatred Prison Moochie was espousing, there were things I couldn't forget. White men wearing badges and guns came to our house on that April morning in 1982. White men had interrogated Moochie without a lawyer. White men put handcuffs on his wrists and shackles around his ankles. White men and women announced to the world Moochie was wanted for murder. White men had given Moochie a pepper spray bath. It was white men who considered putting Moochie to death. That accumulation of events seeded the ground for me to dislike white people. Moochie's words provided the water. That's another layer of the messy reality that is race; extreme personal pain and trauma can convince you to downplay the harm caused by those you love and imagine injustice where there is none. Most of the white people who helped capture, convict, and punish my brother didn't do so to uphold white supremacy; they did so because Moochie had killed someone.

Yet anytime hatred of white people threatened to fully blossom in my heart, I'd come across someone like that ten-year-old boy. Or I'd remember the times Neal Floyd, a white classmate of mine through middle school, and I shared a laugh. My giving in to a hatred of white people would have been a betrayal of Jenee Knight and her parents. She remains one of my best friends in large part because her folks bucked the trend of many other white St. Stephen parents. They refused to take their white daughter out of St. Stephen public schools and transfer her to Macedonia, which is why she was the lonely white face in a sea of black students during our high school graduation.

I'd see white men down at the IGA—the town's main grocery store, owned by a white man who offered me a job in high school—in dirty white T-shirts, darkened by a long day of work under car hoods or in the fields, like the one I was wearing. Ms. Shiver, my middle school English teacher, would pop to mind. She recognized my ability to write long before anyone else and helped me develop it, even though my handwriting was so awful she spent extra time after class teaching me how to type.

She neither ignored nor gave in to my stutter. While Ms. Clarke told the class I would never be a public speaker and let me sit out verbal assignments, Ms. Shiver made sure I completed them. She'd pull me aside and tell me she would call on everyone else in the class in a predetermined order but would let me decide when I was ready.

"Whenever you give me a signal, I'll call on you," she'd whisper to me.

That gave me just enough control of the situation that I could develop an internal rhythm before standing up to speak, a technique that continues serving me well when I climb up on stages today.

In college, I met even more white people who made it difficult for me to embrace hate. While I was having those varied experiences with white people, getting the full range of their humanity, Moochie was behind bars writing letters saying he'd be ready to defend himself, to the death, to avoid being raped, that his primary contact with white people was with the relatively few white fellow inmates and prison guards who felt the need to show aggression to try to maintain order in a place where chaos was king. Moochie's view of the world was stunted by bars and razor wire. When he came into the world, his view was nearly as truncated, for he grew up during an era and in a place where it was routine for white people to put upon his parents and for his siblings to literally walk on ground made sacred by the sweat and blood of slaves.

★ ★ ★

[B]efore a crowd that included women and children, Mary [Turner] *was stripped, hung upside down by the ankles, soaked with gasoline, and roasted to death. In the midst of this torment, a white man opened her swollen belly with a hunting knife and her infant fell to the ground, gave a cry, and was stomped to death.*

That particular lynching occurred in a place called Lowndes County, Georgia, and was recounted in Patrick Phillips's *Blood at the Root: A Racial Cleansing in America*. It occurred a little less than three hundred miles from where my father was born. Those three hundred miles may as well have been three hundred feet, given that it was only one of thousands of such race-based killings recorded throughout the South between Reconstruction and well into the mid-twentieth century.

My father was only a two-year-old boy when Mary Turner and her still-developing child were lynched. Neither age nor gender protected black people against white violence. It's one of the reasons Moochie was unmoved when I challenged him with the image of an innocent white boy, because he knew about all the innocent little black boys and girls who had been stomped to death. Much of his time in prison was spent studying such events while I was being taught in a public school system that had adopted history books written by a proud descendent of a white Confederate soldier.

Moochie knew what Mama and Daddy and Granddaddy had experienced and seemed to grow angrier by the year at the thought of that ugly reality. He was in prison becoming more Afrocentric; I was free but struggling to grapple with the reality that my oldest brother had murdered a white man. He urged me to study what he was studying. I had little interest in following his lead. It never crossed my mind to ask the oldest members of my family what they had experienced, even though we had grown up in the Deep South.

★ ★ ★

My father, the man who ruled our house with an iron fist, would crumble in the presence of white people. As did my grandfather. Each man, whom I knew only as quiet but fierce, would bow not only to white men and women, but to white children, to little white boys.

"Even for the youngest white child, he'd say, 'Yes ma'am, yes sir,'" Mama told me about her father. "I guess it was his upbringing or whatever. And the white chur'n, they would always call him by his name, Bo Diddly."

That is, until my father and grandfather got drunk. That's when they'd beat their wives inside the house and find the courage to defy white people out in public. My grandfather would become well-known for a long rifle he carried around town nearly everywhere, a gun he'd use to shoot my grandmother in front of their kids, wounding, not killing her. She'd later die of leukemia after a life spent giving birth to a dozen children and enduring the abuse of her husband, which got so bad she'd leave the house for several days or weeks at a time.

That's when my family's journey through the criminal justice system began in earnest, though not because my grandfather shot my grandmother or because my father hit my mother in the head with a hammer. They would be jailed time and again for public drunkenness and speaking back loudly to white people in positions of power; and white people oversaw just about everything in St. Stephen.

Granddaddy and Daddy would pay, not only with their bodies, but with at least half of the already-small paychecks they earned from sharecropping, working in fields owned by white men, or low-paying manufacturing work they'd find. Their frequent jailing and legal fines stressed an already-strained family, and there was just about nothing they could do about it. Mama tried anyway. Even as a teenager, she would begin speaking out, trying to find ways to get law enforcement and other city officials to leave her husband and father alone, explaining to them that her family could barely survive because of a revolving jailhouse door that forced them to hand over the little money they spent long hours every day earning.

She spoke to the white police chief and the two black members of the city council.

"I remember talking to some of them," she told me. "It's kind of like, you can talk but you don't have a voice."

She kept talking and ended up in a near confrontation

with the white mayor in his front yard until the mayor's wife pushed him back inside. That was no small thing. When Mama was growing up, St. Stephen and other surrounding areas were so-called sundown towns. The Equal Justice Initiative found that maybe eight in ten of the documented lynchings between 1882 and 1968 happened in the South, and that South Carolina was one of the twelve most active lynching states in the United States.

South Carolina had the tenth most lynchings in the nation, with the last documented mob killing happening on February 17, 1947, in Pickens County. A mob of thirty-one white men grabbed twenty-four-year-old Willie Earle, who had been charged in the death of a white cab driver, beat him, and stabbed him and shot him to death. Most of them admitted to taking part in the crime. Still, each of them was acquitted by an all-white jury; the courtroom erupted in cheers as the verdict was read. Only the white judge and black onlookers were disappointed. Mama was five years old then.

The rumors about why Moochie was in prison that circulated within my family as we struggled to comprehend our potential fate were wrong, even insensitive to the memory of Mr. Bunch and his family. That doesn't mean they were baseless. It was absurd to believe the Mafia had anything to do with our two small Southern towns, not absurd to think powers beyond our control could have been responsible for railroading a young black man in the South, because it had happened so many times before. Willie Earle was one of the most unfortunate ones, the way he died, but his story isn't an anomaly.

The KKK never showed up at our door to exact a kind of revenge for Mr. Bunch's death. But the Klan and its hoodless sympathizers—some were jurors, some were judges, some police officers, teachers, bankers, and real estate brokers—were well-known throughout the South since the Civil War, including in rural parts of South Carolina in areas like ours.

"We were told not to walk after dark in St. Stephen," my aunt Doretha recalled. "Every now and again, you heard of something that happened."

Something like a lynching. Moochie knew that. For a long time, I didn't. Maybe that's why I spent years prioritizing the pain felt by the white family of the man Moochie had killed over the pain felt by my black family.

Maybe that's why I had to go find them.

Denial

While I was pining to meet the Bunch family and empathizing with white people, I was hating black people. "Hate" isn't quite the right word; there might not be one to adequately describe my jumbled, contradictory thoughts and feelings. Hate is as close as I can get. A young black girl who caught my eye had no idea I was struggling with my identity.

She was beautiful. I remember watching her as she stood behind a register at the Food Lion grocery store just down from the McDonald's where I was working part-time. Cover Girl commercial, I thought when I saw her, for I could see her becoming one of those people we read about, discovered by a talent agent who just happened to show up in her checkout aisle.

Her smile was bright, her eyes brown, piercing. Her teeth straight and white, skin smooth. Her dark, shoulder-length hair had likely been straightened with the kind of tool—a wood-handled curling iron—I once took to my own head, burning the tops of my ears, to remove the kinks that have for too long been known in African-American circles as "bad hair."

The girl in the Food Lion vest was my age, about sixteen years old. I recognized her from a school function, maybe before or after a football, baseball, or basketball game I was playing in against her school, Macedonia High, our primary rival. She recognized me, too.

I can't remember why I was in the store. Maybe she told me that's where she worked and I had come up with an excuse to swing by and pick up a candy bar and bag of chips and purposefully got into her line. We made small talk. Somewhere during our minutes-long conversation, she wrote her phone number on a piece of paper and handed it to me.

I was overjoyed at the possibility of love. I could risk it and call her, despite my stutter. Usually, though, I worked around the phone. Or I could simply show up at the store again and ask her to go to a movie at a theater with me.

I did neither, never tried to find out if what felt like a mutual teenage crush was real, for my initial burst of joy gave way to an uglier reality. *Her skin is so dark,* I thought to myself while putting her number in the front right pocket of my blue jeans as I walked out the store.

Man, if I dated her, my boys would laugh at me.

I never saw her again. It wasn't the first time I felt ashamed of black people for being black. It wouldn't be the last. That remains among the most regrettable things I've ever done. It hurt to write these words. It wasn't Moochie's fault, or anyone else's. I don't know why I developed those thoughts. Not every black person who faced what I faced began despising dark skin. Still, while white supremacy clearly imperiled black bodies, it infected infinitely more black minds.

In the South, white supremacy became a systematic attempt to excuse the rapes and murders and lashes to the back. Too many white Southerners—neighbors, those who sat in the church pews next to me, shopped at the same Walmart—were concerned about protecting the image of their ancestors who enslaved my ancestors more than they loved me. They longed for racial quiet more than racial justice and were willing to protect it with their lives and livelihoods, even if it meant committing mass murder in race riots inspired by white anger and hate and designed to reverse black progress. Economists who believe in rational responses to market factors like supply and demand likely haven't studied the South closely enough.

It was hard to grasp that truth while every day being greeted at the local hardware store by nice white people with smiles plastered on their cheeks and Confederate flag stickers (or the real thing) on the backs of their pickup trucks. Where we lived, white developers routinely branded upscale communities "plantation," knowing the word makes it easier to sell homes to wealthy white people at higher prices, not caring what that word conjures in the minds of black residents. That's why there are thousands of "plantations" in South Carolina, including at least one bank, and not one named "concentration camp." Everyone in the South knows a "concentration camp" sign on a development would be beyond absurd, because it would trivialize Jewish pain and be a stark reminder about the historical horror and present-day threat of the Klan and neo-Nazis who targeted Jewish people as much as black people. But "plantation," no biggie.

We were surrounded by friendly white people who celebrated the life of Robert E. Lee, the man who led the Confederate States of America into battle to preserve the institution of slavery, and those who cheered the flying of the battle flag above our statehouse. Speak to most white Americans native to the South, and they'll likely express reverence for Lee. He was a God-fearing man, the greatest general in the history of war, a man so morally sound he led the charge to reunite the country after the Civil War. That's why it should have come as no surprise to anyone paying attention that the removal of a Lee statue in Virginia would cause hundreds of white supremacists to march in Charlottesville and chant "we won't be replaced" during an August 2017 riot in which a young protester was killed and several others injured.

Lee, in their telling, shortly after the war showed enormous respect for black people and challenged fellow white Southerners to do the same by kneeling next to a former slave in a church when other whites wanted a return to slavery, or at least segregation. Much of what they believe is myth built upon a denial of the horrors unleashed by their ancestors. Lee was no friend of the black man; he was a slave owner who believed slavery hurt whites more than blacks, and that God would determine when black people no longer needed to be in bondage.

He had a choice to lead Union troops but instead joined those fighting to establish permanent black enslavement.

Had he won, I and my family would be slaves today. And yet, I have white neighbors, friends, and colleagues who brag about his heroism and battlefield acumen.

"The blacks are immeasurably better off here than in Africa, morally, socially & physically," Lee wrote in 1856 in a letter frequently misquoted by defenders of the Confederate flag to paint him as a man who abhorred slavery. "The painful discipline they are undergoing, is necessary for their instruction as a race, & I hope will prepare & lead them to better things. How long their subjugation may be necessary is known & ordered by a wise Merciful Providence. Their emancipation will sooner result from the mild & melting influence of Christianity, than the storms & tempests of fiery Controversy."

You cannot understand the racial pressures faced by Southern blacks without knowing the myth of Robert E. Lee. Cities such as New Orleans had to protect construction workers as they removed statues built in his honor because to those who love the myth of Lee, such a thing is akin to defaming the memory of George Washington or Benjamin Franklin. The mythical Lee is the personification of the kind of person black Southerners of my generation frequently had to contend with. In debates, I've had white friends respond angrily to my belief that the Confederate flag should not have a place of public honor because it neither represents nor honors us all.

"If we take it down, what else will you want?!" several times white friends, associates, and readers have thundered in conversations with me. The question assumes that public space—paid for by my tax dollars, too—belongs to them, that Southern history and identity must be considered from the white perspective, and, when not, is little more than a perversion thrust upon them by racial agitators and race baiters.

In so many ways, it worked. Growing up, I spent more time bothered and angered by Moochie's talk of kings and queens of Africa and the shortcomings of white people than I did challenging white people who embraced symbols and systems and stories that turned black pain into benign, misunderstood fairy tales. The much-discussed Southern charm was real, and an incredibly powerful and effective way to get black people to wonder if the segregation we were experiencing really was a burden, or if we were simply being overly sensitive about racial slights and should just accept things as they were.

The dark irony is that during the period Malcolm X's radicalness was helping the advancement of civil rights by making Martin Luther King Jr.'s demands more palatable to white people, the threat of the KKK always looming in the recesses of the black Southern mind gave cover to white people who never burned crosses on black people's front lawns but nonetheless provided strong, if quiet, support for the status quo.

Good white people, not overt racists, were the most powerful advocates for Jim Crow *because* they were good. We knew to be highly skeptical of those who sprayed us with tobacco juice spittle while calling us nigger. Those who called us "brothers and sisters in Christ" more easily penetrated our defenses. That's why in too many instances, the corrupted black mind unwittingly joined good white people in their defense of the racially indefensible. My mind was one of the corrupted. That's why I hated my own skin. It was difficult to grasp that truth because the roots of a white supremacy that used our tax dollars to build and maintain monuments and statues dedicated to men who literally lynched our ancestors and openly bragged about the murders were hiding in plain sight.

That's also why the Supreme Court was right in 1954 when it declared the "separate but equal" doctrine bankrupt. Our region first declared whiteness the epitome of intellect and socialization and relegated blackness to a step above the apes. Then they separated us by race. I wasn't old enough to remember the days black people had to move off sidewalks to make space for approaching white people, or go to the back of the restaurant to buy a hamburger or have a white worker retrieve items off the store shelf because black hands should only touch things already purchased, but many of my family members and friends not much older than I am do.

The message was clear. You didn't need to be an adult or in possession of a doctorate to understand its implications. How I saw my dark-skinned would-be girlfriend was part of that legacy. Watching Moochie in chains reinforced that thinking. His imprisonment warped my thinking in ways I'm only now coming to grips with. The sight of silver handcuffs digging into dark flesh leaves an indelible mark. Still, I wonder what was unique about me that made me susceptible to that kind of thinking in a way many black people from the North—and plenty from the South—weren't. Why did what I experienced convince me to love black people less even as what Moochie experienced taught him to love black people more?

★ ★ ★

For a few weeks at the end of my junior year in high school, I stopped avoiding mirrors and was momentarily able to stomach the sight of myself despite a self-image distorted by a stutter, an abusive father, and a 1982 murder. I was preparing to give a speech to become senior class president and was urged, as was every other candidate, to write my thoughts down and practice again and again...and again. The mirror would help me visualize, I was told. I could perfect my posture and hand placement, could determine if the transfer of my eyes from my notes to the crowd was smooth. The mirror could help me track the slow rise and fall of my diaphragm to better control my nerves and watch my mouth articulate each word.

The more I practiced, focusing on every movement, on my cadence, on how to use my arms and stretch my fingers, on finding a rhythm, the easier it would be to deliver the speech, I was told. *Articulation* and *enunciation* were drilled into my head. Exaggerate facial expressions in the mirror; it will be easier to maintain them when nerves kick in onstage, I was counseled.

I did everything my public-speaking teacher told me to. We did not deal with the stutter and the unique challenges it caused. I was treated like every other student. For the first few days of practice, I couldn't complete the first sentence without stuttering horribly, even standing alone in front of the mirror. By the end of the week, I was delivering the entire three-minute speech poignantly, as all the techniques from Mrs. Legree's speech and journalism class were being put to good use. The words that had long flowed smoothly through my head were flowing smoothly through my lips. For the first time, I felt mesmerized by the sound of my own voice. My enunciation was excellent, particularly when pronouncing words ending in "t." My intonation was outstanding, my stance firm and powerful.

★ ★ ★

I was sitting in a blue plastic chair on the stage in the St. Stephen High School cafeteria in front of maybe 300 people, along with a handful of other candidates vying to secure various student body and class offices. I was more relaxed than I had ever been onstage. No doubts.

"These students are vying for elected offices and are about to tell you why they are most qualified," a teacher yelled over a steady hum from a distracted crowd, pointing back to the ten students sitting behind her onstage.

Benjamin, one of my best friends, stood behind the podium first. He was running for student body president. He made witty, confident remarks and elicited a few warm laughs. There were other students, less witty and more nervous, who seemed to be rushing through their deliveries to find comfort in their seats. One candidate stood next to the podium while a friend read her speech. She had a sore throat and couldn't deliver it herself, her friend explained.

Then it was my turn.

"Okay, everybody calm down and give your undivided attention to Issac Bailey, who wants to be senior class president," the teacher hosting the event told the crowd.

I rose from my seat, typed speech in hand, and walked the five feet to the microphone. I sat the thin stack of papers on the podium and adjusted the microphone, my eyes slowly panning the entire audience, from left to right, as I had been taught to do, to portray confidence. My classmates were sitting to my immediate right, the sophomore class directly in front of the stage and freshmen to my left. The seniors were on a field trip.

"My name is Issac Bailey and you should elect me as your senior class president." *Just like in the mirror, smooth, I thought.*

"I, I, I, ah," *slow down, don't rush,* but those reassuring words couldn't slow the pace of my rapidly beating heart.

"I, I, ah, I am the mmmmmm, mmmmmmmm, mmmmmmoooooooosT…"

Students in the audience exchanged dumbfounded glances.

"…qualified pppppperrrr ppppeerrrrssssssooooN ffffffffff fffffffoooooorrrrr…"

The quiet didn't last. A boy sitting in the third row directly in front of the stage had been sitting still as others around began laughing. He knew my eyes were fixed in his direction, though he didn't know I was looking through, not at him. He resisted giving in to the chaos and tried to avoid eye contact with me. He slowly lifted his left hand toward his mouth; his brow began to frown. He was in the thinking man's pose until something snapped. He jerked forward, as if vomiting his amusement about my speaking abilities, and laughed uncontrollably, his head bobbing up and down. Before I was finished speaking, he ended up with one knee on the floor, his left hand over his mouth, his right hand smacking the back of the chair in front of him. I don't know if he wet his pants, but I could see tears of joy well up in his eyes. The day before, I think we were high-fiving each other on the basketball court in gym.

A quick glance around the cafeteria proved he was not an outlier. I could see the same joy on the faces of a few teachers, could hear their bone-deep laughter, as they desperately tried to hide their bemusement while half-heartedly trying to calm the audience of teenagers. Though memories associated with highly emotional events aren't perfect, my description is not an exaggeration. It was that bad.

Almost everyone in that room was black. Almost everyone laughing at me was black. "Hate" is the right word for what I was feeling on that stage. There was no "we are all in this together" sense of comradery. When I took that stage, St. Stephen High was still poor and small and underfunded and almost all black, nearly four decades after *Brown v. Board of Education*. On that day, my stutter segregated me from everyone who looked like me even though we all had been assigned to a relic of the segregated South. Those wearing light skin and dark skin joined for a few brief moments to revel in the reality that despite their common struggles and challenges they'd later face because of race, at least they could open their damn mouths and talk.

A few of my classmates laughed as well, but most were aghast at the response of the audience. They were used to my stutter, had heard me speak that way in class and on trips to the movies. During one such trip, we stopped by a Burger King drive-through. I tried unsuccessfully for ten minutes to order my food over the cackling voice coming through the plastic speaker. I would have sat there for thirty minutes or longer if a friend didn't intervene.

"What?" the fast-food voice interrupted again and again and again and again and again until Carmen, a classmate riding with me, leaned over and ordered our Whopper meals.

"Tell them to hold the mayonnaise," I wanted to say, knowing I'd never eat a hamburger lathered with that condiment, but I kept quiet. My eyes cut through the fast-food worker like lasers. She pretended not to notice.

The audience at St. Stephen didn't pretend. They felt no shame for openly ridiculing me for my stutter. I kept talking, rushing through each speech block, anger spurring me on to stand behind that podium for as long as it took to say every word of those prepared remarks. It took fifteen minutes to complete my three-minute speech, maybe longer. My classmates rose as one from their seats to give me a standing ovation, crowding out the sound of laughter that had engulfed the cafeteria. Almost all my classmates were black, too. It was precisely the "we are in this together" kind of comradery I had heard Mama and my aunts say black people needed, particularly in the South, the kind Moochie was relentlessly advocating from prison. I didn't fully appreciate the gesture. I was too angry. It was easier to focus on those hurting me than those trying to help.

I sat on the stage through the rest of the speeches, silently cursing those who had laughed.

They don't stutter and they are still too scared to get up here. And they're laughing at me?!

That day reminded me of an event from a few years earlier, when I was expected to shine in a regional academic science competition. During practice sessions, I answered every question. During the first round of the competition, I didn't buzz in a single time even though I silently answered every question, afraid my stutter would make it impossible for me to respond within the designated few seconds timeframe. My team lost because of me and my stutter.

"Hey, Ike Ike Ikey, hooowww yoooooouuuuu uh ah uh ah uh doooooinigggggg?" a few students mocked as I walked back to class after my senior class speech.

Shame descended upon me. It cut deeper than the shame that comes with having an older brother in prison, being the son of a man who beat his wife, or being black in the Deep South.

In an odd way, climbing up on that stage, and others before and after it, was an attempt to hide from myself. I didn't have to contemplate who I really was or what I was facing in the rest of the world as long as I could be angry at people for laughing at my stutter. It was the kind of denial that also kept me from openly discussing Moochie. Walking the hall after the speech meant the focus was back on me, and I didn't like who I'd become. I didn't like how I felt, or looked, thought my butt was too big. I didn't like the gentleness of my voice, my attempts to pose as a fluent speaker in front of hundreds, didn't like that I considered not trying again, or that I was made to deal with something as stupid and rare as stuttering. I didn't like me.

The roses and kind words I was given the next day in Mrs. Legree's class were meant to acknowledge my supposed strength, to show that my most influential teacher and friends were proud of me. It was the day the election results were revealed. I became president of the St. Stephen High School class of 1991. I don't remember being happy about my victory. I remember thinking Mrs. Legree and my classmates were proud of a young man I had grown to despise.

I still couldn't talk, was still trapped inside my own damn mouth. And I was still black.

The Other Family

A young black man named James Nathaniel Bryant III had murdered white Horry County police corporal Dennis Lyden on the side of the road. He savagely beat Lyden with his own flashlight, then shot him to death. I was one of the reporters writing breaking news stories for my newspaper during the manhunt for Bryant. I interviewed police officers and residents of the area where Bryant was thought to be hiding, and those who had lived with Bryant and knew him best. And I spoke to a bombastic local NAACP president who wondered aloud if Lyden's death had been the result of racial profiling—suggesting Lyden had improperly stopped Bryant and triggered the deadly encounter—a suggestion that enraged the police and most members of the community still in shock over the death of a man in uniform.

I was there at the end of the manhunt and described to readers how Bryant was captured, how he was taken into custody after being found hiding in a toolshed in a stranger's backyard. I was there when Bryant's father spoke on his son's behalf in court many months later. He passionately argued against his son being sent to death row, a noble but impossible task given that his son had killed a police officer in one of the reddest states in the nation.

His words in that courtroom shook me because they sounded so familiar. They were an echo of the pain I'd detected many times in the words Mama had spoken about Moochie, and eventually about a few of my other brothers. It is horrific to be a parent of a child taken violently; nothing can soothe that anguish. But the sorrow of a parent of a child who has murdered is unlike anything else. You can't grieve, even though you need to because having your child locked away behind bars is a kind of death. You can't run and hide from personal guilt—*what could I have done better; did I unintentionally send a signal to him that violence was okay*—and even your best friends and neighbors and complete strangers will wonder where you went wrong. When parents do a good job of parenting, society has told us a thousand times over, kids turn out right. They won't drop out of school. They won't get pregnant too early or out of wedlock. They won't be bums on the streets begging for change. They will grow up to be upstanding, productive citizens—certainly not murderers—if their parents provide just the right mix of household stability, kisses on the cheeks, and discipline.

I can't count the number of times I've seen Mama try to thread the needle, standing up for her wayward sons, no matter what they did, while making it clear she hated what they had done and empathized with those they had harmed. It's nearly impossible for parents to effectively sell the message that they tried, that they truly cared, when their child messes up. Society refuses to believe that a parent isn't all-knowing or powerful enough to guarantee that their children stay out of trouble. That's why so many parents, and others who love perpetrators of crime, feel relegated to the shadows. That's why they try to cling to a truth many others know little about or don't want to believe—that not everyone who does a monstrous thing is a monster.

Bryant's father was forced to take his pain and shame public to try to save his son's life.

"This is not what me and my family are about," he pleaded with the judge and jury who had just found his son guilty. "If I could give my life so that Officer Lyden could come back, I would."

"I believed him," I wrote in a column for my newspaper.

I did and still do.

★ ★ ★

I was sitting across from Mary Hilton about three miles from the spot where Moochie had stabbed her brother, James Bunch, to death and nearly burned down his little country store a quarter of a century earlier. She sat in a leather booth next to a friend she brought along in part for support, in part to make sure I wasn't a crazed man wishing to do her harm. We were meeting in a small diner a brisk walk from where my brothers and I swam growing up, a place called Bonneau Beach, though the only thing resembling a beach in the area was the soft beige sand on a slit of land protected by massive trees just off Lake Moultrie.

Hilton was elderly, but not old. She was short and thin but not frail. Her pale skin looked as you'd expect pale skin to look after absorbing three-quarters of a century of the Southern sun, but not worse for the wear. She was cautious in the way many of us become as we age, not deathly afraid but keenly aware of her surroundings and the potential dangers they represent, the biggest one of which was a large, young, black, stuttering dude wanting to know more about the murder of her brother.

I had spent the preceding few weeks doing internet and phone book searches and calling up old high school friends to find members of the Bunch family old enough to remember what happened in 1982. I spent countless hours in the Berkeley County Library looking up obits and other sources to find names and places. It was during the period I had finally begun seeing a psychiatrist to face my struggles with PTSD-related visions of violence. I happened upon Hilton's address and phone number during that search.

After the initial excitement of finding her contact information died down, panic overwhelmed me. What would I say to her when I called? That I was a reporter investigating an old murder and the lingering effects of crime, which was true? Or that I was the brother of the man who killed her brother, which was also true? My stutter complicated the already complicated. It's hard enough being the brother of the man who murdered the brother of the woman you needed to cold-call; it's harder still trying to explain why you are calling as words tumble out of your mouth in unpredictable ways, stumbling and bumbling over themselves after the person on the other end of the phone says, "Hello?"

On the day I got up the nerve to call Hilton, I spent time preparing for and avoiding that phone call in equal measure. I picked up the black phone receiver on my desk and slammed it right back down. I picked it up again, punched in the first couple of numbers, then slammed it down again. I sat down and wrote out questions in my notepad with the kind of detail I hadn't in years to feel more prepared. I wandered aimlessly around the newsroom trying to avoid eye contact with my colleagues to prevent getting involved in conversation as I pondered what to do. I walked around the parking lot, went back to my desk, then right back to the parking lot. I visited the bathroom several times hoping to find comfort in solitude and to hide the tears I kept having to fight back.

I've had to make thousands of phone calls during my career and have come up with various ways to compensate for my stutter, knowing the stutter is most pronounced on the phone. I'd send an email first, introducing myself and the purpose of my outreach. I'd call when I knew the person on the other end wouldn't be there so I could speak into the voicemail. That was a few magnitudes easier than having to respond to a live voice, though sometimes I stuttered so fiercely, I'd sit on the phone for half an hour recording and rerecording the same message, hoping to make my voice clear enough to understand. The voicemail lady would hang up on me anyway. There's no odder feeling than knowing you've been rejected by an inanimate object too impatient to listen to you through a stutter.

When I was successful leaving such messages, it became easier to call the next day because I could say, "I left a voicemail yesterday," an icebreaker that worked for reasons I still can't explain, or I'd get a return call and be the recipient, not the initiator, which was easier still. When possible, I preferred driving to the source's office to speak face-to-face or at least leave a business card with a secretary. Often, though, I couldn't rely upon that tactic. It took too much time in a deadline-heavy industry, so I was mostly stuck with expending a lot of mental energy coming up with creative ways to make sure words getting lost between my brain and lips didn't prevent me from putting words on the page.

Those phone interview struggles were most pronounced at the beginning of my career, having to sit within feet of colleagues who freely conducted interviews everyone in the newsroom could hear. Those struggles never went away, though I learned to handle them more efficiently. Just the thought of trying to interview Hilton on the phone flummoxed me like no other interview. A year later, I would expend a lot of energy before another such interview—with Barack Obama during the height of the 2008 presidential election cycle.

I sought solitude in the bathroom a few times and took several deep breaths before that one as well, but not nearly as many times as when I was readying myself to speak to Mary Hilton. I thought about canceling the interview with Obama, not wanting to embarrass myself, though I eventually gathered my nerves. The stutter wasn't crippling when I spoke to him. He didn't mention it. Obama didn't seem bothered by it—I wasn't even sure he noticed it—as we spent time talking health care and race and how he expected to do in South Carolina.

In that case, I went forward with the call because to allow stuttering to stop me from doing a big interview would have felt like the ultimate professional failure, as though I was living down to the paltry expectations so many had of my ability to speak. I was too stubborn to let that happen. The call to Hilton felt more important. It was professional and personal and revealing in ways speaking to Obama could never be. He couldn't shed light on one of the most important nights in my family's history the way Hilton could.

"Hello. Who's this?" the voice called from the other end of the line.

"Um...um...um...hi...um...um...my name is...my naa-aameee...my name is I...I...I...Issac Bailey," I struggled to say, realizing despite hours of contemplation, I still hadn't made up my mind about how to introduce myself, a murderer's brother or a journalist, which further complicated my plans to speak clearly enough to set up a face-to-face interview.

"Huh? Who is this? What did you say?" Mary Hilton asked.

"I'm...I'm...I'm...I'm Issac Bailey and um...um...um...um...I'm looking into the murder of your...um...um...yoooouuuur brother Mr. James Bunch and I'd like to meet with you for an interview."

"I don't want that paper," she said before hanging up abruptly, though not disrespectfully, thinking I was a telemarketer.

I ended up at her house days later after a nearly two-hour drive from my office, trying to do in person what I couldn't accomplish over the phone, efficiency be damned. It was less than ten miles from my boyhood home. A few locals helped me pinpoint the small dirt road where she lived, and I pulled my blue Ford Explorer truck into her front yard. I knocked on the door of her modest brick home several times. She didn't answer. I walked back to my truck, wrote out a note that included my name and number—and that I was the brother of the man who killed her brother—put it between her storm and front doors, hopped back into my truck, and left.

I considered never returning. I wanted to talk to her, to find out more about the family linked with mine for eternity. Shame wanted me to stay away, and my stutter didn't help. As I left, I noticed a small, nondescript restaurant, Evelyn's Diner, housed in a single-wide trailer, the kind you would only find in a town as small as Bonneau, a town where it was truth, not cliché, that almost everyone knew almost everyone's name. The town's population hadn't had a growth spurt in decades. There are probably a thousand pine trees for every resident. The census recorded a 493-person population in Bonneau in 1940, six fewer people in 2010, and only 501 by 2013. It's about three-quarters white. Nearly a quarter of its families live below the poverty line.

I asked the owners of Evelyn's Diner if they knew about the 1982 murder of James Bunch. One of them had and told me they also knew Hilton. A cook told me about a man named Artimus Brinson, a longtime friend of Hilton's, pointed me to his house, and gave me the phone number for the current Bonneau mayor, who was the first emergency official on the scene in 1982. Brinson told me he remembered meeting my mother at Mr. Bunch's funeral.

"Your mother was a real nice lady," he said.

Brinson was an older white man who had trouble walking. He was bearded, plump, and eerily jovial, especially given that we had only crossed paths because my brother had killed Brinson's friend twenty-five years earlier. He was the kind of man Hollywood producers pattern characters after and kids use as the basis for tall tales about the recluse down the street.

His small cinder block house was near busy Highway 52, which ran through the middle of Bonneau. It still stood a short walk from where Mr. Bunch took his last breath. The house was full of trinkets and antiques, bordering on hoarder territory. It smelled of mothballs, mold, damp wood, and stale air mixed with the overpowering scent of an old man who probably needed help to bathe properly.

I liked him. It wasn't the first time I was in a house like his. They are a dime a dozen in our region of the South and are populated by white families and black families alike. Sometimes they are the only option for good people struggling to make ends meet. After we talked for maybe a half hour, mostly about the importance of forgiveness and the uncanny human ability to move beyond hardship, why I was there and how my family turned out over the past quarter century, he struggled to make it to his phone.

"She's seen a lot of tragedy in her life," Brinson said about Hilton as he began to dial.

"There's a wonderful young man here I think you should meet," he said after exchanging a bit of small talk and before telling Hilton I was a young writer and the younger brother of the man who killed her brother. She agreed, meaning Brinson accomplished in a couple of minutes what my phone call and visit to Hilton's house couldn't. A couple of days later, Hilton and I sat down for a ninety-minute interview at Lakeside Café in Bonneau Beach. That's where I found out about and met the Bunch family after twenty-five years of wondering.

★ ★ ★

The Bunch family knew tragedy the way my family would come to know tragedy. Five years before my brother stabbed her brother to death, Hilton's youngest son was killed during a store robbery. His murderer was sent to death row, though his sentence was eventually changed to life in prison. Twelve years after my brother confessed to killing her brother, Hilton's oldest son was found dead and alone in the woods a county over. The person, or people, who murdered him was never identified or found. Hilton couldn't bring herself to speak in detail about how her son was killed. It hurt too much.

For a quarter century, I had been dealing with guilt and shame, and Moochie was adjusting to a new reality where his body was scarcely still his own. My family had been dealing with the aftermath of a murder my brother committed. All the while, Hilton had been trying to cope with having the lives of three loved ones taken unexpectedly, violently, in ways for which there will never be satisfying answers. She was in her seventies when we met, still grieving for her brother and her sons. A week hadn't gone by during those twenty-five years that their untimely deaths hadn't haunted her, hadn't forced her to have to beat back depressive thoughts. Sometimes the thoughts flooded her mind multiple times a day. Sometimes they were unbearable.

"Every day and night I think about my children and my brother," Hilton said. "It never goes out of my mind. It ruined my life. Every day I think about it. If I didn't pray, I wouldn't make it. I have to pray to ask God to ease my heart. That's every day and every night."

"I have to take her shopping to get her out of that mood," Lora Winslow, Hilton's neighbor and best friend, the woman she brought to the diner, would gently cut in every time emotion began to overwhelm Hilton. "She gets depressed about all that stuff, so I go get her and we go out. And we have lunch and shop. Because she doesn't need to stay in that house and think about it. You can't forget. You can't forget."

Hilton rarely opened her front door for strangers; that's why she didn't answer or come outside when I showed up. It wasn't because a strange black dude was standing on her front porch. (Early in my journalism career, when I'd knock on doors in white neighborhoods to conduct interviews, I'd step back several feet before the person emerged to make sure they knew I wasn't there to do harm. It made initiating conversation through a stutter that much more difficult, but it felt necessary. It was one of the many subtle ways I tried to make up for Moochie's dark deed, purposefully going above and beyond to make sure white people were comfortable in my presence.) Winslow had to intervene once when Hilton wouldn't open the door for a furniture deliveryman. A sign on the front of her brick house read: "This home is equipped with an intrusion alarm."

Still, Hilton smiled when we initially sat down in that booth in that diner. I wasn't expecting that. I didn't know if she would hate me, though I told myself I couldn't blame her if she did. We laughed, cracked a few more jokes, and talked almost like a mother and her long-lost son; she was that kind. I told her time and time again who I was, that it was my brother who killed her brother, though I'm not sure why I kept repeating that fact. I wanted to assure myself I wasn't taking advantage of the kindness of an elderly woman, but also found saying it again and again felt like I was paying a kind of penance for the harm my family had caused hers.

Hilton told me about her brother and their family. James Bunch was one of ten children. He was born on Christmas Eve in 1930, about twelve years before my mother. Hilton and Bunch were half of the four youngest siblings. The six others were much older. Only Hilton and two sisters, one in Florida, the other in Macedonia, were still living when we met that day in 2007. They grew up in a shack, an old store just off Highway 52 in Bonneau. They were poor like we were poor, like the bulk of families in Bonneau and St. Stephen were poor.

Bunch loved animals. They had a family dog named Fannie.

"He was just an old dog but he would bite you if you were a stranger," Hilton said.

We laughed again.

He discontinued his formal education in elementary school, though Brinson later said Bunch was good with mathematics. He worked in a shop owned by an older brother in Charleston for several years before opening his own place in Bonneau—the place where he would be killed by Moochie. It had a pool table on which my brother and many residents, black and white, spent several nights playing while listening to music and drinking. Hilton helped him stock the store with snacks, beer, candy, and other convenience items. He left everything he owned to her. He never married, never had children of his own.

"He said his first love married someone else so he couldn't trust it again," Brinson said.

Bunch loved visiting his sister in Florida when he could get away on the weekend. And he loved giving kids free candy and bubble gum and babysat a neighbor's little boy while the neighbor worked. Hilton's youngest son, the one who was murdered in Savannah, Georgia, in 1977, ate his final Christmas dinner with Bunch at his store in December 1976.

For a while, Bunch served as a Bonneau councilman during a time of upheaval in the town. The mayor and a councilman had died, and things were so chaotic the town's lights were cut off. Bunch worked to get them back on and kept the town afloat until the special election could be held to fill the council seats.

"He ran the town of Bonneau for six months and never charged them a penny," Hilton said proudly.

No one I spoke with in Bonneau said a disparaging word about the man my brother killed. The town clerk and the ladies who own Evelyn's Diner had not forgotten his murder. They didn't remember all the details but knew he was stabbed and that it was brutal. That's when people in Bonneau began consistently locking their doors for the first time, they said.

"James (Jim) Bunch has become another statistic in the evergrowing [*sic*] annals of the criminal justice system," a May 5, 1982, *Berkeley Democrat* editorial read. "While at the national level his death will only reflect a number under MURDER, we suspect he will long be the topic of discussion in Bonneau by friends, neighbors and citizens. Years from now, people will still be talking about the crime and the circumstances that led to it."

Hilton, like my mother, didn't understand the circumstances that led to the murder. Brinson said he was surprised because my brother and so many others had laughed with Bunch, had shaken his hand, had been friendly. Though she couldn't bring herself to speak aloud the details of her sons' murders, she was able to tell me about her brother's. She was told Moochie had waited in the bushes outside her brother's shop. Bunch's house was next door. Someone called him out of the house and asked to buy a loaf of bread. As he walked to the store, that's when my brother jumped on him from behind. That's the version Hilton remembered.

She had also been told Moochie was the product of a family of mean people.

"He had to be mean to do something like he did," she said.

Had she known it was my mother and sister she shook

hands with at her brother's funeral, she would have had a few choice words for them.

"I was still bitter," she said.

In the version of the murder she was told, Moochie cut off her brother's nose, slashed his throat twice, cut out his lung. She said there were eighteen stab wounds in her brother's back alone. She was called to go to the hospital. Bunch somehow had been able to stagger to a home next door, where Brinson's father lived.

"He bled to death even before they called EMS," Hilton said.

Mr. Bunch's house was set ablaze, which helped prosecutors decide to bring the early death penalty charge. Hilton doesn't believe my brother set that fire. She didn't like the way officials handled the scene or the investigation, though she didn't want to elaborate.

"I have to live here," she said.

My mother wonders how it was possible for one man to stab another in so many places—in his face, in his neck, in his chest, in his back—all by himself in such a short period of time. Hilton believes Moochie had no help when he killed her brother. That's why she didn't want to talk to my mother or meet my family. It would bring back too many bad memories.

"But I'm glad I don't hate 'em, because hate would eat you up like cancer," Hilton said.

She would not have been in Bonneau when my brother killed her brother had her youngest son not been murdered in Savannah, where she lived happily with her husband for twenty-six years.

"Everywhere I went somebody [in Savannah] walked up to hug me, and it was more than I could take," she said.

"We were very close," she said of her relationship with her brother. "Jim would come and stay with me on weekends in Savannah. I enjoyed talking to him. I enjoyed telling him my troubles. He helped me a lot when [my son] got killed. He would tell me little things that would make me feel a little better."

★ ★ ★

Brinson later called another of Bunch's three living sisters, Malvenia Litchfield, who lived in Macedonia, a few towns away from Hilton, home to St. Stephen High School's primary sports rival. A nephew answered instead. And he was angry, angry that Brinson would call Litchfield to dredge up such a painful past. He told him not to call again, not to bother her.

"He threatened me," Brinson said. Litchfield later apologized for her nephew's outburst, told him she didn't know why he reacted that way.

I was going to leave it there but found Litchfield's number myself and called. She answered. I wasn't as afraid of her reaction because I had already spoken to Hilton and Brinson. She knew who I was—the brother of the man who killed her brother more than the journalist looking into an old murder case—because Hilton and Brinson already told her. That made the conversation easier, the stutter less of an initial impediment.

She told me that Mr. Bunch was a quiet man, that he took care of their parents deep into their old age. She told me she kept a copy of the newspaper story about his murder, and from time to time pulled it out and read it. And cried.

"When I look at that it..." Her voice trailed off. "I feel like he didn't have to die."

She said that though she didn't know who Moochie was she initially wanted to kill him after getting that call at midnight about the murder.

"It didn't change my life. It just hurt me real bad to know that my brother was killed," she said.

She told me that she was sorry for my mother, because Litchfield had lost a son, too.

"Not to prison, but he was killed in an accident," a logging accident at the Georgia-Pacific wood plant in Russellville, where my mother, my stepfather, Moochie, and my brother Josh all worked at one time or another.

Before my brother killed their brother, people bickered about how the police department was handling the area's primary crime issue: cars speeding through the middle of town down Highway 52. That angst, and a lack of funding, led to the temporary shuttering of the police department.

"The chief had to park his car because of it," Bonneau Town Clerk Liz Wren told me.

That's when the murder happened.

"In my short time as the chief of police for Bonneau, this was exactly the situation I was trying to prevent," George Farrey wrote in a letter to the editor in the *Berkeley Democrat* a week after the murder. "If at the time in question Bonneau still had a professional police department, would Mr. Bunch's assailant still have attempted his plan?

Or would he have changed his mind if the Bonneau police car, with that so-much-disliked blue light operating, was writing a traffic summons on U.S. 52?"

Knowing what I know now, that would not have mattered. Moochie was in neither a good place nor a rational state of mind when he approached Mr. Bunch that fateful night. He would not have noticed a patrol car. He would not have cared about a uniformed officer or blue lights, because in those deadly moments, he didn't care about anything. Potential punishment would not have deterred him, not even the thought of the death penalty. He had crossed a Rubicon. The time to prevent that murder had passed long before Moochie picked up that knife and went to Mr. Bunch, because as crazy as it sounds, Moochie never planned to kill anyone.

His clandestine approach at night armed with a weapon suggests otherwise, but only to those who have never sat down and really listened to men who have committed ugly acts and asked them why they did what they did. The sociopath plans and is purposeful. His intent is to harm, to kill, to inflict pain or humiliate, or all the above. With men like Moochie, their irrational thinking convinces them that they can get what they want—he wanted Mr. Bunch to drop robbery charges over a stolen $240—without anyone getting hurt, that the weapon in their hand is a negotiating tool, or something they might need for self-defense if things went wrong. They don't notice what should be obvious, that they are unnecessarily creating the dangerous situation in which a weapon might be used in an unanticipated heated moment.

For the larger society, that distinction is often lost, and most violent criminals are forever judged on the outcome instead of the factors that led to their dastardly deeds. It's a rational response, given that the murdered person is just as dead no matter the cause. And one violent act can unnerve an entire community, as it did to Bonneau, a town not used to such things. Mayor Rembert Wrenn said there hadn't been another murder within town limits during the quarter century since the 1982 murder that changed the course of my family and the Bunches.

The distinction, though—the difference between a sociopathic killer and a desperate or disturbed or broken man who kills—must begin mattering if our goal really is to reduce violent crime and provide justice for victims and their families while leaving open the possibility for the redemption of the wayward. Punishing crime is a necessary evil. But building stronger communities and families requires no longer mistaking punishment for justice.

★ ★ ★

Though my family and the Bunches were far apart, we all grieved. They had to deal with the memories of a loved one snuffed out in one of the most violent ways imaginable; we had to deal with the complicated reality that though we hadn't caused their grief directly, it would always feel as though we had because one of our own did. They moved on, continued to live, just as we had. There was no other choice. A few of them moved out of the area and had children who married and had children of their own. Hilton lived in a modest brick home in Bonneau Beach with a loving husband until he passed away. A sister moved to Alabama, another to Florida.

For a while, Hilton ran a farm with her husband in Dorchester County.

"We ran cows," she said.

She has good memories about how her brother could always make her feel better, give her reason to look to God when she became depressed about the murder of her youngest son. She also had clarity about what should happen to Moochie.

Before I met her, I imagined our families getting together, hugging and crying on each other's shoulders, banding together to free my brother from the prison system that at that point had held him and the rest of us hostage for twenty-five years. Before that, I had desperately wanted to use my journalistic skills to uncover a grave injustice, to prove that Moochie was just another young black man in the South railroaded by a racist system. I wanted to run to Mama to tell her that Moochie really was innocent. It wasn't to be. The facts I uncovered showed he was guilty.

When Moochie called nearly three decades into his prison sentence and finally told me he had killed Mr. Bunch, he said he wanted to apologize to the Bunch family. I was relieved, because it proved his prison-induced fog had begun to lift, and because I was old enough and strong enough by then to handle and crave the unvarnished truth, whatever it was. I no longer needed the lie of denial to keep me sane.

Moochie wanted one other thing—for the Bunch family to speak on his behalf before the parole board, to show him mercy, to help set him free. My family had been hoping for years that Moochie would one day be allowed to come home. During those same years, Hilton and Litchfield were just as certain he should never taste freedom, sure that if he ever did, they would never be able to rest. They hadn't changed their minds in the twenty-five years before we met, or even after we exchanged pleasantries.

"My feeling is to keep him there. Keep him there," Hilton told me without blinking. "He killed an innocent man that wasn't bothering nobody. To put him back out there, he is liable to kill another innocent. I want him there. It would be the best for him, and it would be the best for me if he stayed there."

I understood, though no longer felt shame for wanting Moochie home. Hilton and Litchfield wouldn't have peace if Moochie was released; my family wouldn't have peace if he wasn't. Despite that awkwardness, of sitting across from a grieving woman who just told me she wanted my brother to rot in prison for the rest of his life, I couldn't get up out of that booth before doing something I had been longing to do for years.

"Mrs. Hilton, I know...I know...I know...um...um...um...um...um...I know this won't make any difference, but...I'm...I'm...I'm...um...um...um...I'm...I am truly sorry for what happened," I said, determined to let neither my stutter nor my face flushed with embarrassment stop me from completing my task. "I'm really sorry about what my brother did."

"You couldn't help it," she said, leaning toward me across the café booth, gently cupping my hands. "And neither could I."

I can't remember if we just shook hands or hugged after our two-hour talk. I know it wasn't the Hollywood ending I had long hoped for. No long embrace, no exchanging contact information with a promise to stay in touch. Hilton told me that while she appreciated our conversation, she didn't want to speak to me again, or anyone else in my family.

"I understand," I said meekly before hopping into my truck and driving away.

Maybe ten minutes into a two-hour drive I suddenly pulled to the side of the road, a place surrounded by the tall pines of Francis Marion National Forest. I didn't want to cry but couldn't hold back the tears. And they kept coming...and coming. Maybe fifteen minutes passed before I could compose myself enough to steer my truck back onto the road and head home.

I don't know why I cried. For Hilton. For me. For Moochie and Mr. Bunch and Mama and my sisters and brothers. For St. Stephen and Bonneau. For love, for hate, or out of shame or as a release that was twenty-five years in the making. I hadn't cried like that in nearly a decade, when I had received news that rocked me nearly as hard as Moochie's imprisonment.

A couple of weeks after I had spoken to Hilton, Aunt Doretha walked into a café in Bonneau and saw a poster and a petition on the wall. It said if residents didn't want to see a murderer go free they should sign up and contact the parole board. Moochie's name and photo were on the poster.

"They called him a murderer," Mama said, holding back tears of her own. "They called him a murderer."

It wouldn't be the last time that label would be used to describe a member of our family.

Shame

It didn't matter that Morehouse College had produced Dr. Martin Luther King Jr. It only mattered that I saw a chain-link fence separating the campus from what seemed like an economically depressed community that reminded me of St. Stephen. As soon as I saw it, I knew I would not even consider attending one of the nation's best known HBCUs (Historically Black College and Universities). I noticed the fence as we made our way onto campus during a visit with Morehouse's football coach. We were given a tour, reminded of the school's historic legacy, and shown the football stadium, and we spoke to a few professors. None of it mattered—because I couldn't get the fence and the look of that community out of my mind.

Neither did I consider Howard University, which Willie, who graduated high school two years before I did, was attending. Howard, like Morehouse, was a revered HBCU. Howard, like Morehouse, would have felt like leaving St. Stephen and ending up at a place only slightly less black. I wanted a *lot* less black. Part of my resistance to institutions that produce a disproportionate percentage of black professionals and history makers—Spike Lee,

Toni Morrison, Thurgood Marshall, Zora Neale Hurston—was rooted in my long-distance, evolving relationship with Moochie. It was also because of a white woman I never met.

"An 'A' student at St. Stephen couldn't even get 'Cs' at Macedonia," a white parent at Macedonia High School told a local newspaper.

Her words were embedded in a story about a potential merger between St. Stephen and Macedonia roughly four decades after the Supreme Court had declared an end to separate but equal. Macedonia was maybe one-third black. St. Stephen's collective test scores were low. Our state and national exam results convinced many outsiders we wouldn't be ready for anything other than unskilled labor once we graduated—if we graduated. We didn't have chemistry and computer and physics labs, or access to Advanced Placement classes. Almost all of us qualified for free lunch.

Our parents worked in manufacturing and textiles industries that were shrinking as we matriculated through twelve years of school. As those jobs began disappearing, the battle against illegal street drug sales, and the violence that came with them, began taking root. A desegregated high school with better resources would be a godsend, we thought, if not for us, for our younger siblings.

Then rumors that St. Stephen High students were lazy and violent began circulating. We had fights, like at most schools, but we were safe. We didn't host a memorial service every other week because students were being shot and killed in gang fights. We were more likely to drown swimming at Bonneau Beach than die in a drive-by shooting. Still, that white Macedonia mother argued we weren't good enough to be among white people. She didn't want us to infect her children.

Her words affected me more than Moochie's preachings about black self-worth.

★ ★ ★

I wanted to strangle Andy. He and I were teammates on the Davidson College football team. He was a good guy. I respected him. We were sitting in the first-floor lounge of Belk dorm on the campus of the elite, mostly white private college a short drive from the New South city of Charlotte, North Carolina. I fell in love with Davidson the moment then–Davidson head football coach Dave Fagg picked me up for a visit. It was as though someone had read my mind, discovered my thoughts about how a college should look and feel, and used them as a blueprint for Davidson. There was expansive green space, and oaks and pines and Spanish moss. A fraternity row, a new athletic facility, and a building full of classrooms that seemed straight out of a Gothic architecture magazine greeted me. Redbrick sidewalks and co-eds sunbathing and playing hacky sack and Ultimate Frisbee on the grass as though the place was their birthright were in abundance.

It was the center of a small town not much bigger than St. Stephen but was everything St. Stephen wasn't. I wondered what that white mother from Macedonia would think of one of those dumb, unprepared black St. Stephen students being invited to such a place. I wondered what Moochie would think, though never bothered to tell him where I had gone. During my four years at Davidson, I spoke about that white mother several times, telling classmates how she motivated me, particularly when the issues of race and culture shock became topics of discussion. Not once did I mention that my oldest brother was in prison serving a life sentence for first-degree murder.

I was sitting in that Belk dorm lobby with Andy near the end of my first year and the first night of the Rodney King riots. We watched the images of burned buildings, police officers in riot gear, and angry protesters and looters on CNN, mostly black people responding to the acquittal of four white police officers who had been caught on video beating King bloody.

It had been a difficult year for me. The reality of Davidson's reputation had hit me hard on my first review (the word for "test" at Davidson), in Psychology 101, and never let up. The school prided itself on academic excellence and expected every student to embrace that ethos. It was rumored that professors commonly practiced a kind of reverse grade inflation; the fewer As the better. The highest-scoring student on that Psych 101 test had earned a 98, the professor told us without divulging student names. The average was an 88.

"The lowest score is a forty-eight," he said. The class erupted in an audible gasp.

I was that 48.

There I was, the number four graduate of the St. Stephen High School class of 1991, living up to the negative images that had dogged us for all those years. It hurt more knowing that an ex-girlfriend had warned me not to come home "too white"—meaning having adopted the cadence of white students, their dress, thought, and life outlook—while the 48 meant I was becoming too stereotypically black.

Psych 101 had about twenty-five students, a large class at Davidson, whose student body numbered about fourteen hundred. I was the only black student in a sea of smiling white faces. As I discreetly folded my test and quickly stuffed it in my book bag, too ashamed to look the professor in the eye as he handed it to me, I could imagine that white Macedonia mother shaking her finger in my face, saying, *Told you so, nigger.*

My classmates bantered about the hijinks they had planned for the weekend. I pretended to banter along with them, nodding my head approvingly to everything they said, trying to mask my secret, a Scarlet 48 buried deep in the book bag slung over my left shoulder. They were white. I was black. They were smart. I was dumb. Their smiles were real, mine a façade. Their presence at Davidson natural, mine a cosmic joke turned tragic. That failing grade was compounded by an injury on the football field, a partially torn hamstring, that kept me sidelined for much of my freshman season. Life seldom let me overcome one seemingly overwhelming challenge before sending another my way.

On most nights, I trapped myself in the dorm room for fear of failing out; that is, when I wasn't trapped in the athletic trainer's room performing excruciating rehab on my leg, which I tackled with such a relentless passion I was dubbed "Iron Ike." (I shortened my name to Ike at Davidson because it was easier to introduce myself to new people that way. Sometimes I'd go the James Bond route, saying my last name first because "Bailey" was easier to say without a stutter.) I felt in control of little else, but fixing my leg only required hard work and a solitary focus, something my stutter and dealing with the aftermath of Moochie's imprisonment had taught me long before.

When you fail out like so many black college students do, I imagined my white classmates saying, *your brother will have a warm bed for you next to him in prison. Don't drop the soap. Nigger.*

It was the scariest day of my life. My mother would be disappointed, I thought, as would Mrs. Legree, that a prized black student had gone off to an elite white college only to become another in a long line of affirmative-action flameouts, even though my high school resume didn't read like someone's who had been given an undeserved handout. My high school GPA was nearly perfect. I was a National Honor Society student and senior class president who juggled academics and part-time work at McDonald's and participation in three sports. None of that mattered as I cried on the bed in my dorm room.

So what that my mother and stepfather were caring and unrelenting and had shown me the way to success; that teachers had instilled in me the ability to endure and given me a strong educational foundation, despite the shortcomings of our school; or that my academic exploits included membership in Who's Who Among American High School Students and being a role model for a younger sister and brothers. The words from that white Macedonia mother kept banging inside my head, trying to convince me a St. Stephen High diploma amounted to little more than a participation trophy. As I stewed on her words and that 48, I began pulling away from Moochie more rapidly. The letters I had been writing him became less detailed and fewer and further between until they slowed to a trickle, then dried up completely.

It hurt too much to think about what he had done and where he was, but also what it suggested about me. During a period in which I needed him to convince me that we really were kings and queens from Africa and had provided the foundation for every modern-day invention, no matter how embellished those claims, I was busy crafting a life that purposefully excluded him. I was so successful in cutting him out of my life, I was left virtually defenseless when I was forced to stare at that 48.

I desperately needed Moochie to protect me from those new bullies, like he had done with the old ones so long ago. The bombardment came from seemingly everywhere—from the white female classmate who sat in our dorm saying it was unfair that black students had been allowed to attend Davidson.

"*They* aren't prepared," she said, careful to exclude me and my black roommate from her analysis.

Then there were the white students who wrote in *The Davidsonian*, the college's weekly student newspaper, that black people had no history of success and had to make things up to feel good about ourselves. It even came from the Jesse Jacksons and Al Sharptons, who made it sound as though without affirmative action black students had no shot at real-world success. Black conservative writer and professor Walter Williams piled on when he told black parents to not let their children attend schools where they weren't within one hundred points of the school's SAT average. My score was nearly three hundred points below Davidson's.

I pulled it together by neglecting my social life and adopting the attitude I used to survive long hot summers in St. Stephen–area tobacco fields I worked. Those fields and those days felt endless. I got through by putting my head down, ignoring the length of the rows and the black tar building up on my fingertips, and focusing on each plant and the bottom three leaves I was instructed to meticulously remove from each and place in a collection tractor. I stopped noticing the pounds of sweat building up in my T-shirt and pants. After a while, enduring triple-digit, or nearly triple-digit, weather from 6:00 a.m. to 6:00 p.m. five days a week no longer felt impossible. I began treating each class assignment at Davidson the same way, not allowing thoughts about what my blackness meant—or the difficulty of the task—to get in the way.

By the first semester of my sophomore year, I was earning a 3.3 GPA and a spot in the starting lineup on the football team after my hamstring healed. (Looking back, I'm sure I would have done better, and sooner, had I embraced the kind of group study and consistent interaction with professors more successful Davidson students had. I was too ashamed to have studied smarter, not just harder.) Before that transformation, I was sitting in Belk dorm with Andy, still unsure if I was worthy of Davidson.

The riots sparked discussion on campus, but not nearly as much as when O. J. Simpson, a black NFL Hall of Famer, would be found not guilty of killing his white ex-wife and her friend a couple of years later. Sitting in Belk on an almost-all-white campus watching black men and women on CNN run and ravage their neighborhoods, fire and smoke and darkness providing the background, my spirit was uneasy. Andy and another white student sat on a couch near me. Each spoke easily about how we were witnessing mindless self-sabotage.

"They probably desensitized the jury to that videotape by showing it over and over," they said of the defense lawyers. "They probably dissected it to pieces. I can see how they reached that verdict. Rioting over it? Ridiculous."

How could they watch the video—a man lying on his back on the side of a road trying to block several minutes of blows from batons and boots—and conclude not guilty was a reasonable verdict? My blood began to boil.

"You can't tell me this doesn't show how fucked-up our justice system is," I shouted, without a hint of stutter. "Why does the rioting disturb you more than state power being used to beat a man nearly to death?"

"Rodney King was on PCP, and we probably didn't see the whole tape," Andy answered. "Think about the dangers cops face and the effects PCP can have on a person, it seems reasonable."

"You saw that tape!" I yelled again, trying to keep my sentences short to not awaken the stutter. "You saw that tape!"

"That tape isn't as clear as some people are trying to make it seem."

"You saw that tape, man. You saw that tape," I said a few more times, but the fluency sparked by my anger had begun to subside. I desperately wanted to say more, but was afraid my lips, tongue, and jaw would let me down. I wanted to ask why two intelligent young men could so easily swallow injustice without so much as blinking.

I wanted to tell them we all understand the danger a police officer faces, that he must be allowed to use the force necessary to subdue a suspect—but never more. I wanted to say that with a gaggle of officers on the scene and Rodney King on his back, beating and stomping him was police brutality of the worst kind, that not even animals should be treated that way.

A not guilty verdict in the face of evidence like this is reasonable from neither a legal nor a moral perspective. It's criminal to be okay with this outcome. Can't you see this will just increase the level of distrust between black communities and the police who are supposed to be serving them? How can that be good for either side? Cops are empowered to uphold the law, not be above it.

If they could only hear those thoughts making their way clearly through my mind, they'd reconsider, I tried to convince myself.

It's not happenstance that we've had racial disparities within the justice system since it was created and that black men, who have long been perceived as uniquely violent, animalistic, even, have always—always—been on the wrong end of those disparities. When will our voices, our experiences, count at least as much as a white cop's fear?

I wanted to say all of that but said nothing. Once again, I had failed to escape the prison of my mouth. After shouting "you saw the tape" a few more times, I slouched back into my chair and swallowed my anger, which made me angrier still. I knew many Davidson students, those who would soon be making decisions that would chart the course of our future, held similarly dismissive views about King's beating.

That's when I began regretting my decision to ignore Morehouse and Howard. At either of those institutions, I probably could have sat back and listened to healthy debate about race and crime and police brutality without having to participate. At Davidson, I began longing for the warmth of the black community I grew up in but never appreciated. I was angry that stuttering beat me into silence. My frustration boiled over later while reading *The Davidsonian.*

★ ★ ★

A black Davidson staff member visited an area grocery store. Two young white men standing behind the counter ignored her, she wrote. They had judged her black skin and weren't willing to treat her fairly because of it, she reasoned, though she swallowed the slight instead of making a scene, a decision black people make every day when forced to contend with incidents they can't prove are about race but don't want to ignore. In response, a white male student wrote to *The Davidsonian* arguing that black staff member was being overly sensitive and couldn't have known the cause of that poor service. Maybe they were just lazy or having a bad day, he argued. White people sometimes receive poor service, too, but don't resort to blaming it on racism, he wrote.

A couple of other white students wrote to condemn her as well. They detailed every possible motive for the service—except racism—and essentially told her to shut up and stop searching for racism in every little slight. The grocery store, a few minutes' walk from the heart of campus, was invaluable to students who didn't have cars, they wrote. Blanket, unwarranted charges threatened that service, they reasoned.

Those arguments were made by some of the most privileged young people in the world. They had been born into the right families, with the right skin tone, at the right time, in the right place. And yet, they felt compelled to dismiss the concerns of one of the few professional black staff members at Davidson. It was as though I was back on that couch in Belk dorm with Andy.

After a few days of apprehension, I submitted my first column to *The Davidsonian,* using a voice that had long lain dormant inside me:

...Whites don't have to look for the derogatory glances that blacks have to look for. Whites don't have to be concerned about hidden agendas in the actions of people of another race. This is the White-American luxury. White people in this country simply don't have to worry about those things because they don't affect them the way they affect African-Americans.

This luxury is not a negative thing; it's probably extremely positive. Hell, if I had it I could probably put all my energies into other things, like studying and going to class and falling in love.

I'm not saying this because I want sympathy; I'm saying this because I believe that there needs to be a whole lot more sensitivity towards those of a different race.

I am sensitive to the fact that White-Americans have this luxury, and that they are not necessarily racist because they don't see the things that I do. But at the same time, I want White-Americans to try and see things from my point of view as well...

For the first time at Davidson, my voice reverberated throughout campus, bouncing off classroom walls and in countless conversations among those mostly white fourteen hundred students, faculty, and staff, and members of the surrounding community. It was a rush to be heard, to no longer feel invisible. Moochie was still writing me letters. Though I rarely wrote back, the strength of his words jumped off the page and spurred me on. I didn't need stories about the black kings and queens of a bygone Africa, after all. The kernels of truth buried in the ravings of a black man in prison were more than enough. They energized me. Though I was keeping Moochie at arm's length, his power was steeling my spine. His voice was convincing me to use my own. Not only that, but in ways I had not yet realized, the stutter had so compromised my self-image it inadvertently freed me to write nakedly. Sharing your deepest thoughts in public, offering yourself up for criticism, thoroughly exposes a person. Because stuttering had made me feel naked all the time, I forgot I was supposed to be afraid of the criticism and ridicule that resulted from my writings. I had faced and felt helplessness every damn day and had survived.

Surviving had so blooded and battered and bruised me, it had become as difficult to *see* my true self as it was to *see* Moochie in those bloody clothes. Readers marveled at my openness—an openness they didn't know was made possible by my battle with a severe stutter. It was like living without nerve endings, leaving me vulnerable to unforeseen threats, but also, as Ernest Hemingway said, able to sit down at a typewriter, open a vein, and bleed on the page.

My voice began showing up in that column even as speaking in front of crowds (and on the phone) remained among my most challenging stumbling blocks. Fighting off thoughts of racial inferiority in a sea of white faces was tough and tiring. Fighting the stutter was ten times as hard.

Dinner invitations from strangers began pouring in, followed by messages from Davidson students, and their parents, about how they were forced to consider the world anew because of my words. That writing success complicated my on-again, off-again quest to improve my speech. Stuttering had no place in my writing, so there was little use in challenging it head-on. My words had broken free from the prison of "disfluent" speech through a loophole. I didn't need my lips and tongue to bend to my every command if I had a pen and a pad.

That writing success convinced me I no longer needed to deal with the years of hurt and pain and scars stuttering had caused, even though my speech and a murder that happened when I was a nine-year-old boy were forever linked and influencing my thoughts and behavior. I was being heard. But the dean of minority students gently urged me to visit a speech therapist in Charlotte.

★ ★ ★

The therapist was impressed by my outward confidence. She went over the well-known anti-stuttering tactics Ms. Starks had several years earlier, easy onset, modified breathing, and whisper techniques. It improved my fluency a bit, though not enough to convince me to keep investing time to try to eradicate the stutter. Writing had become my voice, my world opening with every new column in *The Davidsonian*:

> *...We don't want to be bothered with someone else's problems or viewpoints. We don't want to be "belittled" by someone else's pride. We don't want anyone else to seem more important than we are. And this is why we can't talk.*
>
> *Instead of listening and learning from one another to broaden our thinking, we would rather ridicule and force others to conform to our ideals. Instead of craving honesty, we crave comfort. Instead of recognizing and respecting our differences, we would rather ignore them. Conformity cannot be the answer to our problems because we have too many differences that cannot be ignored...*

My voice had begun intimidating people who had intimidated me. That voice, it just kept springing from me almost against my will. My sociology professor, one of the few black people on Davidson's faculty, threatened to fail me if I didn't speak in class. I had a voice people needed to hear, she said.

I began speaking in her class frequently, as well as several others, and even gave a two-hour presentation on the AIDS epidemic. Never, though, did my speaking prowess come close to the power harnessed by the column. People were often disappointed to hear me speak after they got hooked on my columns. It mattered little, to me, that my fingers banging on computer keys were more eloquent than words flowing out of my mouth. It seemed to matter a lot to everyone else.

When panel discussions about race and discrimination were convened, I was usually asked to participate. The columns convinced others mine was an important voice for those wanting to understand the "black perspective." Never mind I was at Davidson in part because something ugly my oldest brother did had convinced me to want to be less black. Never mind that I didn't understand what being "black" meant, or that I couldn't shake my secret regret of not pursing a relationship because I thought my would-be girlfriend's skin color was too dark. To the public, I was unapologetically confronting the confounding issue of race in a way that sometimes challenged, sometimes disturbed.

Not everybody bought in. I wrote a twenty-page research paper comparing the effectiveness of Martin Luther King Jr. and Malcolm X, coming down on King's side, just as I had done at St. Stephen. In high school, a white history teacher declared that no one in our class could do a Black History Month project on Malcolm X because he had called white people "blue-eyed devils." I followed her edict while many of my classmates wrote about Malcolm any way.

"If I was a black man, I'd be angrier than you seem to be," my white Davidson professor wrote on the margins of the Martin-Malcolm paper under a B+.

A black Davidson student—a friend—called me a sellout, said I was "white" after I penned a column reminding readers that white cops had tough, dangerous jobs and should be respected and not presumed to have ill will in their hearts toward black people. A white professor didn't like that column either, particularly because I wrote it a week after detailing how a black football player had been stopped and his car searched for no good reason in Davidson, a piece that sent a charge through the campus and alumni and parents who contacted me. It wouldn't be the last time I would be praised for highlighting black pain and injustice, then scolded for being too deferential to "the other side."

One of my white teammates was equally unimpressed with my black bona fides. He drove a black Jeep with the kind of expensive rims most commonly seen on tricked-out cars in rap videos. I drove a blue Chevy Nova with slightly upgraded rims, the most expensive I could afford—the cheap five-star, chrome variety. He drove around campus with the Jeep top down and blasting gangsta rap from powerful speakers. He dated black women and was loud and boisterous and more likely to hang out with our black friends at nightclubs than I was. Though he never told me directly, he made it clear in a thousand subtle ways he believed himself more authentically black than me.

I bet, I said to myself on a day he was particularly annoying, he'd change his tune if I told him about how my oldest brother had killed a man, how that murder was among the top reasons I spoke with a severe stutter. I suspect he would not have wanted to trade places with me when I was growing up in a tin can of a house and attending an underfunded, segregated school in an area whose soil was rich with the blood of slaves, some of whom I could trace back to a couple of generations before my mother's. Maybe he would have passed on the days I experienced long before being accepted into Davidson when I hid in the corner of our trailer as my father beat my mother, or the days to come in which neither the depth of my character nor the quality of my work or work ethic would be enough to overcome people's doubts about me and my black skin and my severe speech impediment.

I know—I *know*—he would not have wanted the extra burden, not only having to do the seemingly impossible academic work at Davidson, but also silently trying to knock back thoughts of black stereotypes if I slipped up, just once. He wanted the trappings, the easy stuff, the cool stuff. He didn't want to be black, especially not black like me, because he had no idea what that meant, and I could tell he didn't really want to know. I was getting tired of white people telling me all the reasons I didn't match up to the image of blackness they had rolling around in their minds, and he was the last straw.

That anger accompanied me when I joined four other students and a professor for a panel discussion about race in the student union. Each of us gave an opening three-minute speech.

"My naaaaame is Ike Bailey. I'm, I'm, I'm, um, ah, from this small town called St. Stephen, South Carolina. Um, ah, um, ah, um, ah, I think, ah, ah, ah, um, um, ah, I was in, in, in, invited to speak because of, um, ah, um, ah, um, ah, um, ah, ah, ah, the column I write.

"I'mmmmm, I'mmmm, um, ah, um, ah, um, ah, um, ah, ah, ah interested in this topic, well, um, ah, um, ah, um, ah, um, ah, um, ah, um, ah, ah, ah, because I'm black, and I, I, I, I, I, I think I, um, ah, um, ah, um, ah, um, ah, ah, could add some important pppppppppppeerrrrrrr ppppppperr-rrrr pppppppppperrrrrrrrssspective."

Those people are in the audience to listen to me, my ego quietly egged me on.

Brian, a fair-skinned, dark-haired Davidson student, was staring my way. Every time I stuttered, he stared. I'd speak of the need for affirmative action, dribbling out barely coherent sentences. He'd stare. His uncomfortable-ness with my speech angered me even more.

What the hell is he looking at?

I didn't consider that he was wondering why words didn't flow smoothly from my mouth. It didn't occur to me to empathize with him, given that stuttering made me so uncomfortable I could barely stand to hear my own voice. It didn't register that those who rarely heard anyone speak like me would naturally experience an initial discomfort, no matter how attentive they wanted to be. The warped self-image I had developed because of the stutter freed me to write with abandon but blinded me to the presence of people who genuinely wanted to know why I was different, not to make fun, but to better understand.

"This one is for Ike," Brian raised his hand. "Why do you talk like that?"

"If you don't like what I'm saying, you can just leave. I'm not going to shut up," I shouted at him.

Like Brian, many others in the audience had perplexed looks, some gazing inquisitively at others the moment the static from stuttering flooded their ears. They were all uncomfortable, all trying to pretend not to be. Brian, who agreed with many of the points I was making, was the only one to ask directly about my stutter. I lashed out because denial was still my medicine of choice. His words had penetrated my defenses. And it hurt for the first time in a long time.

A year earlier, as I was speaking at an athletic banquet at St. Stephen High, having been invited back because I was a "good role model," I was growing angrier by the minute as a man in the audience squirmed and contorted himself throughout my twenty-minute speech. He finally got up and left. As he walked out, my voice grew louder, my eyes burned through his back, as if to chase him out the door.

How dare he not listen to me! How dare he not accept me!

I was feigning courage by standing onstage challenging everyone else to be better—while too terrified to commit to improving myself. Neither Brian nor that man at the athletic banquet was being disrespectful; they were just convenient scapegoats. Had I been stronger, I would have responded to his inquiry with the seriousness it deserved. I wasn't.

My white English professor was right. I wasn't angry enough about racial horrors being visited upon people who looked like me. My biggest struggle was my stutter, not my skin color, even when I lied to myself about that reality. I wrote about race because I believed it the right thing to do, but also because it was easier than having to explore how stuttering had changed the trajectory of my life.

While I was traveling that winding road to find my true voice, Moochie was losing his.

Trapped

The only Davidson police officer killed in the line of duty in the 180-year history of the small town in North Carolina was a white man named Mark Swaney. I had recently left Davidson College and had moved four hours away to South Carolina when a friend called to tell me about that 1997 Christmas Day shooting.

I cried myself into the ground, an Earth-shattering, Earth-shaking weeping. My arms went numb, my legs hung limp. I crumbled onto the floor, overwhelmed by grief like I never had before—because the cop killer I loved had also been killed during that shooting, the bullets that killed him and Swaney flying in opposite directions before reaching their intended targets.

The cop killer's name was Damon Kerns, though I knew him as Damon Williams. I first met him during a summer enrichment program at Davidson College called "Love of Learning." He was one of several dozen promising high school students invited to campus. I was a camp "counselor-mentor." *The Charlotte Observer* described him this way in a December 30, 1997, article:

As hundreds of family and friends gathered for the funeral of a teenager who died violently, the Davidson mayor called on the town to bond together and never let such a tragedy strike again. Close to 500 people battled falling snow and slushy roads Monday to attend a service for Damon Frederick Kerns, 18, who was shot Christmas Day during a scuffle that left one Davidson police officer dead and another officer wounded. Officer Mark Swaney, 26, was fatally shot in a struggle with Kerns after the teenager fired on him and another officer. The killings happened in Kerns' west Davidson neighborhood as horrified friends and relatives watched.

Several weeks earlier, I was sitting white-knuckled in the passenger seat of my 1995 green Saturn sedan as I tried to teach Damon how to drive a five-speed manual—or more accurately, I gave in to his sly demands that I let him try—hoping he wouldn't strip my gears clean or get us killed. We drove around town, the car herking and jerking and sputtering along the entire five-mile route until we ended up at his house on the other side of the railroad tracks. It was the mostly black part of Davidson where many of the college's staff members lived, the place where I was told some Davidson professors and other professionals dared not drive through at night even though it was the quickest route from Interstate 77.

I didn't go inside Damon's house. We shook hands and exchanged a man hug, interlocking hands and forearms on our chests to prevent a full embrace. I jumped into my car and drove off, fully expecting to see Damon again, maybe reading a newspaper article ten years later to discover he had become mayor of Charlotte or started a small business that had begun taking off. I knew he was troubled. Still, it wasn't fanciful thinking to expect that future for him. He was too smart not to make it, smarter than me. I knew about the four arrests *The Charlotte Observer* mentioned in the article about Damon's funeral.

He pleaded guilty to assault and disorderly conduct after an October 1996 incident that left a school employee's arm broken at North Mecklenburg. This year, he was arrested on charges of disorderly conduct, obstructing an officer and carrying a concealed weapon. He pleaded guilty to the first two charges, and a trial on the third was pending when he died.

I also knew he was one of the most articulate young men I had ever known. I was the mentor, the guy who had made it out of a tough environment into a privileged existence at a premier institution of higher learning. Still, I was quietly jealous of the way Damon could command any room he walked into. His contemporaries wanted to follow him, and so did a few of us in the older set. It's hard to pinpoint how or why, but when I hear people say Bill Clinton can make you feel like the most important person in a room full of dignitaries, I thought of Damon. He had that kind of light. It oozed out of his every pore.

Only looking back did I realize I was drawn to Damon because he was Moochie in every way that mattered. Maybe that's why I cried, because I had spent my entire time in college denying the existence of my hero older brother—even when I played basketball with inmates at a prison for young men near Charlotte as part of my work with Davidson's branch of the Fellowship of Christian Athletes—and he showed up in the form of Damon anyway.

Those who eulogized Kerns remembered his active involvement in the church, which he had attended the Sunday before his death. They remembered his athleticism at North Mecklenburg High School, where he played football and basketball. And they remembered his work at Davidson College, where he was a service worker and participated in its Love of Learning enrichment program for young people. "Damon was a fun-loving person who was warmhearted and loved helping others. He had a special way of speaking with the elderly, who adored him," read the funeral program. But some speakers, including his cousin and uncle, warned against the troubles that had plagued Kerns. They urged the congregation to rise above the problems of drugs and violence. "When you get in those tough situations, I want you to think about Damon," said cousin Kevin Whitley. "You can do and be whatever you want to be, but it's up to you."

Maybe I cried because it hit me I hadn't done enough to prevent Damon's life from ending too early or before he could do real damage, or maybe because I had little control over his fate even if I had been more dedicated. There were a handful of students at Davidson, black, white, and Latino, mostly young women, who dedicated extensive time and effort to reach those like Damon. Though I had worked myself into such a good academic rhythm I had time to do more, I did just enough mentoring to look good on a resume.

I should have let him drive my Saturn more even if he screwed up every gear, I berated myself. *I should have shaken him until he had no choice but to listen.*

His death, and his killing a police officer, proved I had not found the right words, didn't provide the right example. While I was failing Damon, I was failing Moochie, too, allowing shame to stop me from helping Moochie maintain a lifeline to the real world. Truth is, I felt helpless. I had grown convinced nothing would work, that some of us, particularly young black men, were doomed. It mattered not that I had supposedly proven that foreboding wrong.

Moochie was talented but his impressive brain was rotting away in a prison cell. My youngest brothers had begun walking the path Moochie had blazed. Despite the successes Doug and Willie were stacking up or the fact that a black man—my stepfather, Harris "Boss" McDaniel—had entered our lives when we needed him most and married Mama even though she had a houseful of young kids, I had bought into the notion that black men were lucky to reach our twenty-second birthday aboveground and not be in handcuffs and an orange jumpsuit.

Maybe I cried because I knew Moochie wasn't the only one of my brothers Damon resembled, maybe because I knew what happened to him could happen to them. And I knew if it did, people who only knew them through newspaper headlines would want to believe they were soulless monsters. They'd want no mention of their complexity or the factors that shaped who they had become or why they did what they did. That's what happened to Damon in death. Outraged readers bombarded *The*

Charlotte Observer because the newspaper dared write about Damon and the wonderful things family members and friends had to say about him. The paper, while providing front-page space to Swaney's funeral, the kind of attention every police officer killed in the line of duty receives, noted Swaney had just come off suspension for wildly shooting into a neighbor's home when he was off duty. Mentioning the imperfections of a fallen hero was out-of-bounds, according to *Observer* readers.

In 1982, when Moochie killed Mr. Bunch, it was clear we were expected to shut up, at least publicly, no matter how much we loved Moochie or were grateful for all the times he literally saved us in ways large and small. In 1997, that message was repeating itself. In each case, a black man I loved had killed a white man beloved by the public.

The black sheep of the black sheep mustn't say good things about "bad" men who do awful things. That would be too much like condoning violence, defining down decency. It would be insensitive to the victims and their families. The more hideous, the more one-dimensional black men who kill or physically harm others are portrayed, the better. It's easier to hate them that way, to dismiss those who love them and justify building more prisons and not care if they are raped or murdered behind bars. And if they are monsters, they likely come from monstrous stock, meaning the broken families from which they hail aren't worthy of the resources needed to repair them.

Never mind that we lived in a region where white men who had systematically raped and killed black people were openly honored every day, and in a country whose currency featured the faces of slave owners. Celebrating those white men wasn't condoning violence, defining down decency, or an affront to the victims and their families. It was righteous. It was American.

★ ★ ★

I can't remember how many years had passed before I made my way up to Bennettsville in 1998 to see Moochie, only a few weeks after I pulled myself off the floor of Tracy's apartment and stopped crying about Damon. Tracy and I had known each other for eight years by then after meeting at the South Carolina Governor's School for Academics and had gotten engaged after an off-and-on relationship that had finally gotten serious and committed. The prison was about a two-hour drive from Myrtle Beach. I was a fresh-faced reporter, a glorified calendar clerk. It was a step up. I had been juggling two part-time jobs. I would spend five or six hours on one end of a Myrtle Beach mall in a little red vest, black bow tie, white shirt, and black slacks picking up trash in a movie theater alongside teenagers, then change into a different vest and work several more hours in the Kmart sporting goods department. The work wasn't challenging, and neither my stutter nor having an older brother in prison mattered. In the newsroom, they both mattered.

My having just read Nathan McCall's *Makes Me Wanna Holler* didn't help. The book initially gave me a touch of paranoia as I walked into a newsroom of mostly white journalists. In his book McCall, a former *Washington Post* writer, had described in detail his struggles with race in the professional world as a black journalist.

Which one of these white people do I have to watch out for? I wondered to myself.

But race quickly took a backseat to my stutter. Speaking, and speaking with confidence, seemed to be the rule throughout the newsroom. That's why my first week was hell, sitting at a desk within earshot of several reporters, calling businesses to update "The Beach," the paper's weekly calendar of events for tourists. My desk phone was not even an arm's length from Mike's. He was the guy who had been designing and reporting for "The Beach" but was about to be promoted to a full-time arts writer. Our desks were connected to a few others. A brown partition separated us from another row. Things felt tight. I didn't have the luxury of sitting in an office alone, with time to catch my breath and manufacture the nerve to make yet another phone call, as had been the case at Davidson when I was an intern after graduating.

When I made those phone calls, sweat dripped from my palms. My heart felt as though it was trying to escape through my chest. Sometimes the person on the other end of the line, usually a manager or receptionist, would gently hang up a half second after answering "Hello" and not hearing an immediate reply, not knowing I was in the middle of a stutter and couldn't get a word out. Sometimes I'd be greeted by an answering machine, try to leave a message, and that, too, would hang up on me in the middle of the muddled message I was leaving.

"Um, ah, um, ah, um, ah, um, um, ah, um, ah, um, this is, um, ah, um, ah, um, ah, Ike Bailey, and um, ah, um, um, um, um, um, um, um, um, um, um, um, um, um, um, I'm calling from um, ah, um, ah, um, ah, calling from *The,* um, ah, um, ah, um, ah, um, ah, um, ah, um, ah, um, ah, um, um, calling from *The,* um, *Sun News.* Um, ah, um, ah, I need to get your, um, ah, um, um, um, um, need to get your um, um, um, um, um, need to get your um, um, um, um, um, um, um, need to get your um, um, um, um, um, um, daily hours of operation, and um, ah, um, ah, um, ah, um, ah, um, ah, um, ah, um, ah, um, ah, um, ah, need to double-check on your admissions prices for um, ah, um, ah, um, ah, um, ah, um, ah, um, ah, um, ah, um, ah, um, ah, um, ah, um, ah, um, 'The Beach,' a weekly publication for area events and activities."

"I didn't understand what you said," a startled manager would say. "Can you repeat it?"

The calls were draining, one after the other. A few of the voices on the other line laughed, some nervously, some thinking a friend was playing a practical joke. I'd have to call the same place back two, three, four times to gather information while everyone around me was busy typing into their computers, chatting effortlessly on the phone, or holding loud conversations in other parts of the newsroom. It was humiliating.

Every day I was terrified of being overheard, thinking a colleague, convinced I could not do my job effectively, would report me to a supervisor. Every morning I walked into the newsroom wondering if that would be the day an editor would tap me on the shoulder and ask me to leave. I was so concerned about how best to navigate my stutter I spent little time pursuing assignments that make young reporters stand out. That's who I was when I told my editor I needed a day off in the middle of the week to see my brother. I had accomplished nothing. I wasn't about to volunteer that I had a big brother in prison. I already felt unworthy.

"What do you guys plan to do?" she asked.

"Not much."

"I hope you guys have fun."

She was thinking we might hang out in Myrtle Beach like tourists, maybe take a few laps around the go-kart track at NASCAR SpeedPark, tour Broadway at the Beach, or visit Ripley's Believe It or Not! I didn't tell her there would be no visit to Crabby Mike's because my oldest brother was a convicted murderer serving a life sentence.

I wasn't ready to talk about Moochie but was eager to see him after having spent my college years unwilling to even let classmates know he existed. Tracy and I were engaged, and I needed her to meet him. She needed to get a glimpse of what she was stepping into. I was hoping it wouldn't affect our plans but wasn't sure it wouldn't. If I struggled with Moochie and prison and murder and how those things had transformed my family, why wouldn't she?

I desperately wanted things to be normal, not quite sure what that meant.

★ ★ ★

Tracy and I were sitting silently in a dingy room at Evans Correctional Institution when two guards ushered Moochie, dressed in an orange jumpsuit emblazoned with SCDC on the back, into an adjoining closet-sized area to remove his handcuffs and iron chains and the leather holders that bound his waist and ankles. Moochie had been in solitary confinement for more than three years by then, since the South Carolina Department of Corrections during the Governor David Beasley era instituted a dress and safety code for prisoners, requiring every prisoner to have closely cropped hair and clean-shaven faces. Mtume was a Rastafarian. Growing his hair to its natural length was a sacred ritual. As best we could determine, he was the last one in his prison still in confinement because he refused a haircut. About two dozen other prisoners initially resisted the grooming policy and joined Moochie in solitary, which meant that, for a time, it wasn't really solitary. It was double-booked, stacked with Rastafarians and Muslims and a handful of others resisting The Man. They created a kind of fraternity, supporting each other, encouraging the youngest prisoners, sticking to vows of silence in the presence of guards.

One by one, though, they'd give in, get a haircut and get back into the general population, mostly after weeks or months of letters and calls from family members and friends eager for their visitation rights to be restored. Moochie wound up alone in a dank cell room for four more years after Tracy and I visited, with little light and less human contact. In the Bailey family, it's often hard to tell if someone is motivated by an unmatched strength or unmatched bullheadedness. Moochie likely lasted that long before giving in because he had an abundance of both.

For a while, I naively thought his being in solitary was a kind of favor, keeping him away from the dangers that came with being among hundreds of men locked up together for years on end, from potential rape and other kinds of assaults. It was the one romantic notion about Moochie's confinement I held on to, that he was willing to stand up for something important, consequence be damned. I now know solitary can lead to pronounced mental illness and is a kind of torture. Interacting with Moochie during that visit left little doubt about that.

"I learned how to meditate for hours a day," he told me years later. "If not, you can go crazy. I remember the times I *was* crazy. You go in and out of it."

When Tracy and I visited, his first parole date was approaching. Being in solitary meant he had no chance of earning good time. He could not do the things that make a prisoner look like he's ready to rejoin society, taking college courses or coordinating spelling bees with twenty-five-dollar prizes to encourage younger prisoners to value education.

He smiled when he saw us but dared not speak in front of the guards. I didn't know silence had become his weapon of choice, particularly after he vowed to never arm himself with a shank, afraid he'd use it. He had been using hand signals and head nods and the written word to communicate. Tracy was taken aback. It had to be jarring staring in the face of a crazy man who looked very much like the man she was about to marry. I was taken aback, too. Moochie wasn't Moochie. I doubt he knew who he was. His long, lean, muscular body was still there, topped with dreadlocks flowing halfway down his back. So was his Crest-white smile, caramel-colored skin, and that sly smirk. Whatever else he was inside that once beautiful brain, I wasn't sure.

I wonder what Tracy is thinking about this, I said to myself.

While the guards hovered nearby, including a short black woman sitting in a metal chair in the door reading, trying to give us as much privacy as possible, Moochie barely opened his mouth, instead scribbling on a few sheets of paper, his hand moving like the arm of a seismograph recording the energy of a massive earthquake.

Once we were alone, he spoke, his voice barely rising above a whisper.

"So, he *can* talk!" I heard one of the guards say to the other.

When I tried to get him to speak more, he just smiled bigger. When another guard hovered around, a pudgy white man, Moochie started writing again on small slips of paper that seemed to be falling apart from overuse, ink on the front and back and in the margins.

Moochie's handwriting was barely readable, the letters tiny, bleeding into each other.

"They don't give us too much paper, you know," Moochie whispered and smiled, his eyes darting up toward the guards, then quickly back down. "Those cats something else man. Those cats somethin' else!"

I don't remember anything else he said, or what else I asked, though I suspect he talked about Afrocentricity. As he spoke, I had one eye on him and the other on my watch, hoping the visit would end. I had done my premarriage due diligence. I wanted out of that prison and away from whatever it was Moochie had become.

As he spoke, his torso and head were in a perpetual rocking horse motion, his eyes darting up to us, then to the guard at the door, then down to his paper, the cycle repeating itself in one seamless loop as quickly as his hands moved along the weathered piece of browning paper that had been carefully folded and refolded again and again. It went on that way for about forty-five minutes before the guards took him back, rewrapping the handcuffs around his wrists and the shackles and chains around his midsection and ankles as Tracy and I went back through the metal doors and out of the razor wire fencing.

She knew my family had been talking about ways to prepare him for his parole hearing.

"You honestly think he's ready to get out?" she asked as we headed home.

I let her question linger in the air, keeping my eyes on the road and hands on the wheel.

New Beginnings

Every day walking into the newsroom felt the same. I was overwhelmed by fear and afraid someone would discover that fear. I began covering family fests and the kinds of everyday assignments my more accomplished colleagues didn't want. My stutter made even those tasks difficult to complete. I did just enough to not get fired.

A random call from a reader during a Saturday shift when I was in charge of answering the main newsroom phone changed everything.

"There's a big RV fire off King's Highway down from Third Avenue South," he said. "It looks like the family is out there without a place to stay. Y'all might want to check it out."

The reader had actually only seen the hull of an RV that had been burned two weeks earlier but hadn't yet been moved. When I arrived, two men were sitting on the steps of a bank near the vehicle. They were dirty—caked-on, layers-deep dirty. Their hair was bedraggled, lying down and standing up on their heads in convoluted patterns. Their T-shirts were brown and stained. Their jeans were in tatters. Their sneakers seemed fresh picked from a nearby Dumpster. They smiled when I asked their names.

"Man, we just watching the cars go by, man," one of them told me while letting it slip they lived on the streets.

"Y'all been out here long?" I said.

"Man, we always out here. We been working all day. We takin' a break now."

"Are, um, y'all gonna be around here tomorrow afternoon? I want to talk to y'all."

"Sure, come on back. We'll be around, man. No doubt."

I'm not sure why, but for the first time I thought about rushing back to the newsroom to pitch a major story. A few weeks earlier, I had overheard the news editor say he'd love to see someone tackle a project about the homeless in Myrtle Beach. Before that, as we prepared for the potential onslaught of a hurricane, I heard him suggest that just about every reporter in the newsroom was ready to tackle such an assignment—everyone except me. I knew he was wrong but also knew I hadn't proven myself. Meeting two homeless white men shook me from my stupor. I pitched the story.

"Okay, do it," the news editor told me, I suspect, because every other reporter was busy.

* * *

David, forty, and Joseph, thirty-seven, were brothers who had been homeless for about four years. Combined, they made about sixty dollars weekly doing odd jobs for a handful of residents and businesses. They slept in a seldom-used public restroom in Myrtle Beach with sixty-year-old Lloyd, an alcoholic high school dropout.

Their existence was simple, walking around all day, completing a few errands for people who sometimes paid as much as five dollars. They slept under ragged covers and sleeping bags that smelled as though they had been slept in by homeless men who hadn't showered in years. They dodged the police; their work money was used to buy alcohol and food they'd ration, usually sharing a slice of bread and mayonnaise, and a piece of bologna when they got lucky. They ravaged Dumpsters; Burger King's was a favorite.

David was the most engaging. Walking along the streets, he paused frequently, bending to retrieve pennies from the sidewalks. He had become expert at looking down, cherishing little things most people ignore or consider trash, a damaged radio, maybe a piece of worn cord. Each was a potential barter item, sometimes fetching as much as ten dollars in trades.

"You may not understand," David told me, "but every little thing you get is important."

He was a high school graduate and once made good money as a carpet installer and co-owned a condominium in Florida, but made his way to Myrtle Beach to find his brother Joseph. He ran out of money, he said, and couldn't afford a ticket home. A convenience store manager would eventually buy bus tickets for both men, and a few weeks after my meeting them, they had vanished. Several hundred like them remained in the area.

Some were on the street because they made their way to Myrtle Beach, lured by the promise of plentiful jobs. They were so close to the economic edge, one car breakdown, a blown tire, seemingly small things, left them without money and food.

In the city's homeless shelter, I found stories of drug addictions and alcoholism and a lack of education. Some found their way there because of grief over a lost loved one, others because of a disorientation caused by Alzheimer's and other forms of dementia. There were also couples who had been robbed of all their money and women who had been raped and small children born to crack-addicted mothers and pregnant teenage girls shunned by their parents.

On the streets, a colleague and I, photojournalist Janet Blackmon Morgan, spent weeks tracking down homeless men and women who slept in wheelchairs, on cardboard boxes under bushes near Myrtle Beach City Hall, and in covered parking lots. They found it hard to hide from police because of the glare of constant light from the abundant amusements that attracted millions to the tourist hot spot every year. None of them seemed bothered as I stuttered through invasive questions about their personal lives. They just listened.

We hung out with Lloyd, who was still sleeping in the same public restroom he had shared with David and Joseph. He described himself as an "*old* sixty-year-old man," too old to work, too bothered by long lines to walk to the shelter. His hair was white and thinning. His hands were toughened, scarred from years of farming tobacco and working in cloth manufacturing. His belly hung ominously far over his belt, making him seem more sickly than overweight. He walked with a slow, drawn-out glide, a kind of involuntary shuffle.

His left pant leg had a small hole just below the knee and several strands of string dangled from the ends of his leg cuffs. The worn pair of blue jeans, the T-shirt he wore, a few blankets, a tent, and some other clothes were all he owned. He confined himself to a two-block radius of tennis courts, movie theaters, car washes, restaurants, and Dumpsters.

"I wish I never picked up that first beer when I was a teenager," he told me.

He had made a series of other mistakes, including leaving a good woman, he said, then the warmth he had found after the divorce in the Georgia home one of his sons provided. Still, he insisted he had found comfort on the streets.

"I love it," he said in a barely audible voice as he stared at the pavement.

His body, he said, had adjusted to getting only one meal per day. A manager at an area pancake house would sneak him breakfast food.

"My friend, Mr. Albert, feeds me just about every day," he said. "Albert's a good man."

"God's been good to me," he told me while recounting the times he watched other homeless men leave for good or be arrested for indecent exposure while he was spared.

"This...this is my home," he told me while pointing to the metal park bench he was about to sleep on during a fifty-degree night. "Home."

Every night just before the lights from nearby tennis courts grew dark, he'd say a short prayer, again thanking God. He thanked God so many times each time we spoke, I began wondering if his prayers were just a way to convince me not to think him an abandoned pet.

"The streets ain't that bad," he told me repeatedly, something I heard from other homeless people as well.

I didn't believe him but didn't want to say I thought him a liar.

"If a family member came and picked you up today," I asked, "would you go?"

"Yes," he quietly answered.

Sometimes to survive chronic, dispiriting struggle, you convince yourself that's what you want and even need. I've seen domestic violence victims, prisoners, and stutterers do it. That lie—what doesn't kill you will make you stronger—gives you strength to make it through another day but can keep you forever trapped, blind to better possibilities. It's true that what doesn't kill you will make you stronger—but only if you make it make you stronger.

★ ★ ★

The three-day series on homelessness led to my first professional journalism awards. I suddenly had credibility in the newsroom. I left the busywork of "The Beach" behind. The more the words on the page spoke for me, the less of an impediment my stutter became. In some cases, it became an unlikely asset. Reluctant sources opened up to me in ways they wouldn't for non-stuttering journalists because, I think, the stutter made me more relatable and less intimidating. A few media-savvy local personalities asked my editor if I was stuttering on purpose to receive sympathy after interviews in which they told me more than they had planned.

John X. Miller, then the managing editor, pulled me into his office.

"We've been talking about you moving into full-time reporting," he said.

"Yes, sir."

"We want you to be prepared," he said, twisting a blue-top ink pen between his fingers as though to ease into something he didn't know quite how to say.

"The editors have been talking about your speech. Please don't get me wrong, we don't have a problem with it. But if you got some help for it, it would make your job that much easier. I think your interview subjects would be inclined to take you more seriously."

My heart sank. I said nothing.

"Listen, we know you can do the work. Hell, you already have. If you want help with it, the company will make a way to provide it. If you don't, it won't affect your status here. Just think about it, search for a few programs you think might be helpful, that might edify you. Then come to me and we'll discuss it."

"Okay."

I told Tracy what John X. said, asked what she thought.

"Maybe you should look into it," she said before quickly turning around to fiddle with a pot on the stove that didn't need tending to.

Over the years, I had asked her questions about my stuttering, about how it sounded, about how others were responding to it and why she had initially allowed it to be a hindrance in our relationship. Her college friends would laugh when I called her dorm room. She wasn't sure she could love a joke, especially given that she was struggling through her own self-esteem issues. We had gotten through all of that long before John X. sat me down. Still, the questions I asked her about my speech weren't really questions; they were my way of testing to see if she truly had let go of her shame of my stutter.

That night, though, I just wanted truth.

"So, um, um, um, um, um, ah, um, um, um, ah, you think I should, um, um, um, um, um, you think, um, um, um, you think, um, you think, um, you think, um that I should look into it?"

Several months earlier, she had taken money out of a retirement account to buy a device for me that resembled a hearing aid. It was designed to provide stutterers an audio feedback loop, to mimic what happens during group singing, when stuttering disappears. It didn't work for me.

"Maybe it's time," she said, still fiddling with the pot on the cold stove. "If they're going to help, why not?"

I wanted her to tell me that stuttering wasn't holding me back from anything important, that people hardly noticed. It had taken so many damn years to love myself for who I was. Entertaining an offer of therapy felt like a kind of self-betrayal, as though I was throwing away all that hard work to reach self-acceptance.

Why now? I had finally moved past this damn thing, I thought to myself while beating back tears. *Why should I look back, I'm making it? This is who I am. This is who I am!*

Though it remained my most dangerous enemy, stuttering had become my closest friend. It was there when I cried and laughed and loved and hated and was afraid and felt strong. It was there when Moochie left and Tracy wasn't, gave me insight into people I otherwise would not have. It inspired me to begin writing. Besides, countless previous attempts to rid myself of it had all failed. Stuttering had already proven it would never let me go.

"Listen," Tracy said, this time staring into my eyes, her hands gently caressing my waist. "No matter what, I'm going to love you, okay? Nothing's going to change that. I'm sorry I wasted all that time before. Stuttering or not, I'm going to love you. But don't ever sell yourself short because you are scared. Remember, I spent years doing that, and look what it almost did to us. You know what's right. You decide. I'll still be here to hold your hand. I love you."

★ ★ ★

I sat in the in-take room of the Pee Dee Speech and Hearing Center watching little boys and little girls and their mothers mill around as I waited to get the speech evaluation required by the newspaper's health insurance plan. The place was decorated like an elementary school, bright colors, childlike pictures and drawings on the walls, friendly therapists who could pass for kindergarten teachers.

"You are here for an evaluation, is that correct?" a smiling woman asked me.

"Um, yes. I need it for um, um, um, um, um, um, um, my insurance."

"Your insurance? May I ask why?"

"Um, sure. They said, um, they said, um, they said, um, they said, um, they said, um, that I need one before, um, um, um, um, um, um, um, um, um, um they would, um, consider paying for, um, um, um, um, um, um, um, for this um, therapy program, um, um, um, um, um, um, um, um, um, I'm trying to get into."

"Have you had much therapy before?"

"Oh, yeah."

"What kind?"

"I know about the um easy onset, um, um, um where um, um, um you are supposed to make sure your um, um, um, lips and tongue and jaw are um, um, um relaxed so you can sort of um, um, um so you can sort of um, so you can sort of um ease the words and try not to um, um, um put much pressure on them. And then the um, um, um, and then the um, um, um and then the um prolonged speech, where you um, um, um, um stretch the sounds way out soooommmmmmmettttthinnnnng like that. And I've had that um, um, um machine, that um auditory feedback, and breathing exercises."

"Sounds like you've had a good bit. Do you know much about stuttering itself?"

"About as um, um, um much as I could. The theories seem to suggest that it is um, um, um that it is um, that it is um, that it is um genetic, and that boys um, um, um get it four times more than girls, probably because boys um, um, um mature later, so girls can um, um, um adjust more quickly to things if they um, um, um go wrong early in their um, um, um, speech. And they say that um, um, um sometimes it's a result of um, um, um some kind of early emotional um, um, um, trauma, and my oldest brother um, um, um, my oldest brother um, my oldest brother went to prison when I was real young."

"I think you know just as much about stuttering as I do.

Okay, then," she said, nodding. "Let's get started. I want us to start with a reading sample. What's that book you're carrying?"

"Um, the, um, *Invisible Man.*"

"Can you read a few passages from that while I take notes, unless that will bother you?"

"Um, um, um, um, um, um, um, that's fine. Um, um, um, um, um, um, I am, an invisible, um, um, um, um, man. No, I am not a spook like, um, ah, um, ah, um, ah, um, ah, um, ah, those who haunted Edgar Allan Poe; nor um, um, um, um, um, um, am I one of, um, um, um, um, your Hollywood-movie, um, um, ah, um, um, ah, um, ah, um, ah, um, ah, um, ah etc. um, um, um, um, um, ecto um, um, um, um, um, ectoplasms. I am a man of substance, of flesh and bone, fiber and liquids—and I um, um, um, um, um, um, might even, um, um, um, um, even be said to possess a mind. I am invisible, understand, simply because um, um, um, um, um, um, um people refuse to see me..."

"I think we can stop there. Now, let's talk for a few minutes, so we can get a feel for your conversational speech. I'm curious. Why did you become a reporter? I imagine you have to do a lot of talking?"

"Good question. I'm not um, um, um, um, um, um really sure, but um, um, um, um, um, I love to write, and um, um, um I love to meet people. Stuttering um, um, um, stuttering um, um, um stuttering did hold me back for a while, though."

"I think that fact alone makes you amazing. Most of the adult stutterers I've treated, though I mainly deal with kids, most of the adults shy away from speaking at all. Some don't dare use the phone."

"Believe me, um, um, um I understand that."

It was the most relaxed speech I had in weeks. To my ears, my speech was so free-flowing, I was convinced the therapist would say my stutter was too mild to qualify for intensive therapy. A week later, her evaluation arrived in the mail.

"Issac Bailey is an ambitious young adult who stutters severely. He would greatly benefit from an intense therapy program, considering his personal drive and willingness to deal with the condition," her evaluation read.

"That's wrong," I told Tracy. "That lady doesn't know anything about stuttering."

"Are you sure? Maybe she saw something you didn't."

"She's wrong! I know what a severe stutterer sounds like, and it's not me. I've been speaking this way for almost two decades now. I've studied this stuff; you know that. I know that I'm a mild stutterer. She got it wrong. Wrong!"

I didn't stutter once as my voice kept rising.

"Well, okay," Tracy said before abruptly walking into the other room.

We sent that evaluation letter, and a supportive note from my primary doctor, to the HMO. They quickly denied my request to go to Roanoke, Virginia, to participate in a nineteen-day program at the Hollins Communications Research Center.

My stutter, they determined, was a preexisting condition.

I thought that was the end of it, especially when John X. moved to a larger paper in Detroit. But a new executive editor, Patricia O'Connor, found a way to get the company to pay half of the three-thousand-dollar fee, while Hollins picked up the rest when I agreed to document my journey through the program for *Good Morning America*. (It never aired because of an Egypt Air crash, the coverage of which took over the airwaves.)

I still wasn't sure I wanted to go. After stuttering for more than seventeen years by then, I had grown comfortable with my condition, though never comfortable with myself. My greatest fear was no longer facing daily ridicule, but that those who knew me would find out it still bothered me. Tracy gently pushed. She was no longer ashamed, she said, and neither should I be.

"It came into your life for a purpose," she said. "But it's time to let it go."

★ ★ ★

The first morning of the program in Roanoke, clinicians at Hollins spoke with a certainty I needed at the time and freed me from years of wondering if there was any real connection between Moochie's situation and my own.

"There is no evidence that stuttering is caused by emotional trauma. It is primarily a physical disorder," Ronald Webster, founder and director of the Hollins Institute, told a silent lounge filled with fourteen adult stutterers anxious to begin the intense therapy. "The public perception is seriously flawed."

Dr. Webster spoke about other theories, about the possibility of a genetic link, or even how stuttering may be caused by the density of a stutterer's skull.

"We receive sounds in two ways," he said; "one is through vibrations that are caught through the ear, and the other is the energy that flows through our skulls. That's your silent voice, because it can't be picked up on a tape recorder and only you can hear it, and it is why we all sound different on a tape than we do to our own ears.

"The silent voice in stutterers may travel at a different rate than it does in fluent speakers because of this skull density difference," he continued. "Research suggests stuttering has a hereditary component. A 'stuttering gene' isn't likely, but genes that determine the size, shape, and density of mechanisms involved in speech development may be the culprit.

"As of today, stuttering continues to be a speech disorder without a known cause, nor known cure," Dr. Webster said. "There are therapists [who] try to create happy stutterers, or those who accept their condition as a part of who they are without feeling a need to challenge it. But stutterers can be trained to produce fluent speech."

Since then, a few gene mutations have been identified and are believed to contribute to the development of stuttering, as well as environmental factors and differences in the brains of those who stutter and those who don't.

Therapists at Hollins taught stutterers how to properly move the diaphragm while breathing and to reduce the stress placed on the vocal folds, and retaught clients about the basics of speech production. The program is designed to first teach clients everything needed to produce fluent speech, such as the correct placement of the lips, tongue, and jaw. Clients are retaught how to make single, simple sounds before being moved into complex conversational settings.

"We've learned there are specific movement details that will produce fluent speech—rebuild the distorted movement patterns," Dr. Webster said. "The client does all the detailed speech reconstruction process. But we don't have all the answers, we are still looking."

We were given stopwatches before being introduced to voice-sensitive computers. It takes the average speaker two-tenths of a second to speak one syllable. We were instructed to slow ourselves down to two seconds per syllable.

"My name is Issac" became "Mmmmmmmmyyyyyyyy nnnnnnnnnnnaaaaaaaammmmmmmeeeeeee iiiiiiiiiiiiiiiissssssssssss Iiiiiiiiiiiiiiiisssssssssssaaaaaaaaaaccccccccc."

Speaking had to be done that way while using the full-breath target, the glue for the entire program. Inhale while pushing the diaphragm out, they told us, until we received a comfortably full breath, but not too much, and not too little. When you reach the comfortably full level, let your diaphragm naturally release the air. It is on that release you begin voicing your words, they coached. Don't hesitate—not for a split second—between your inhalation and exhalation and when you begin to speak. If you are off by a fraction of a second, your vocal cords will close, making it impossible to create fluent speech.

"This will be the way you will breathe for the rest of your life," LuAnn, my therapist at Hollins, said. "It's a more relaxing and efficient way to breathe because it eliminates all the shallow, rushed breathing many stutterers have grown accustomed to."

"Be precise," she coached. "Concentrate. It'll take time to get used to it. More than one hundred twenty words, which include about five hundred individual sounds, are spoken by the average speaker every minute. Because there is so much room for error, identifying and correcting the smallest, most basic details of speech are even more important for stutterers."

Slowing down wouldn't produce fluent speech, but it would force precision, LuAnn said.

Dr. Webster warned us about the need for precision when trying to master what they called speech targets. There was a way to breathe by moving your diaphragm, a proper sequence to engage your lips, tongue, and jaw, they said, and once those movements became precise, fluent speech was guaranteed. They had discovered that stuttering occurred because the speech mechanisms were out of place and moving in an incorrect pattern.

When I was there, about four thousand stutterers had walked through the doors of Hollins in the previous twenty-seven years for the intensive therapy. According to their records, more than 93 percent left with normal levels of fluency. About 75 percent maintained that normal fluency for more than two years, and most retained it permanently. Another 15 percent retain significant improvement over their pretreatment speech fluency, though outside the normal fluency range of 3 percent or less disfluencies.

"Emotional stress and nervousness may play a role in adult stutterers because of the years of this repeated, distorted pattern and discouragement at failed attempts to get better," Dr. Webster said. "But in true practical terms, it is all about the incorrect movement of the speech muscles."

It worked for broadcast journalist John Stossel, who has hosted a variety of TV news shows and programs over the past few decades.

It worked for me, too, but not in the way I expected. I was in the 93 percent who left the institute with a normal level of fluency. I was not in the 75 percent who made it at least two years at that level. I'm not even sure I'm in the 15 percent who retained significant improvement "though outside the normal fluency range of 3 percent or less disfluencies."

Hollins didn't free my tangled tongue. It didn't clear the way for me to become a broadcast journalist, as my therapist suggested it might. It freed me in other ways. Because of Hollins, I no longer see my stutter as a friend or a foe.

I want to speak as freely as most everyone else does. I hate knowing its presence this late in my life is connected to a murder over which I had no control. But I learned enough at Hollins to more confidently give speeches and presentations during which my stutter is an afterthought for me and my audience. I know to never again try to mimic fluent speakers. I use hand gestures, not just to punctuate a point, but because it establishes a full-body rhythm that allows me to produce fluent speech. It's why I am likely to walk from one side of the stage to the other several times while speaking and why I often hold a pen in my left hand and request a microphone that is attached to my ear or shirt instead of one planted on a podium.

Ever since Hollins introduced me to the idea that the mechanics of speech can be used effectively to produce free-flowing speech, I've been toying with ways to tailor that concept to my unique circumstances. It's why you'll frequently see me drag an old-school flip chart onstage. When I bump up against a hard speech block, I've learned that just walking over to the flip chart and writing the word frees me from the stutter. All the while, the audience is convinced I wrote the word down to emphasize a major point, and I play along and adjust as many times as necessary to keep my rhythm while never letting the theme of the speech get lost. That's why I only take notes and a bare-bones outline with me onstage. Doing more would rob me of the flexibility I need.

Hollins didn't cure me, like Ms. Starks didn't cure me, like the therapist in college didn't cure me, like a private therapist, Sandra, I met shortly after college—maybe the most impressive speech therapist I've ever met—didn't cure me. It was Sandra who introduced me to an editor, Cliff Harrington, at *The Charlotte Observer*. They were friends and attended the same church. She knew I was a writer and convinced Cliff to give me a chance to prove myself, which I did by writing an article that was featured on the front page of North Carolina's largest newspaper. I'm not sure I would have come across Cliff, or Bob Meadows, another black journalist at *Charlotte*, who voluntarily gave up a writing assignment so I could do it, had it not been for my stutter. Sometimes the universe works in mysterious ways. For months after Sandra worked with me—we'd visit local fast-food joints and I'd practice new speech techniques while ordering at the front counter or in the drive-through—I barely stuttered, if at all. My public speaking began taking off and I began connecting with audiences like never before. While that months-long fluency didn't last (it was a godsend), the confidence it provided me and the journalism connections I established remain among the most important developments in my career.

I learned, though, that you don't have to simply accept your plight in life, no matter the difficulties you face; nor do you have to reach Nirvana to be successful. Sometimes compromising is the best way to hold on to your principles, even when it feels like a self-betrayal.

Not long after I left Hollins, Moochie was forced to learn a similar lesson.

Africa Can Wait

"You honestly think he's ready to get out?"

Nearly two years had elapsed since Tracy asked that question, and I still hadn't answered. I couldn't. All I knew was that I wanted my family's prison nightmare to finally end, and that meant Moochie coming home. Little else mattered. That's why early one morning I jumped into my green 1995 Saturn to attend his first parole hearing.

Moochie would get his chance before the South Carolina parole board in early August 2000, along with seventy-eight others who had been convicted of a range of serious offenses: two counts of armed robbery, grand larceny, and an escape; kidnapping, criminal sexual conduct, and burglary; voluntary manslaughter; aiding escapees from prison and two counts of violent burglary; trafficking cocaine. And murder. One by one, they'd be walked into a dimly lit room but wouldn't sit a desk away from parole board members like in *The Shawshank Redemption.* They would make their case staring into a large monitor. Video images of the parole board members were broadcast into the room via closed-circuit TV.

A few years before that hearing, a life sentence in South

Carolina became a life sentence without the possibility of parole. That stricter law didn't apply to Moochie because he was convicted before it was implemented. Still, no more than 5 percent of violent offenders in the state were being paroled then. Parole had mostly been granted to the sick or those with other mitigating circumstances. A man had been freed a week earlier after serving thirteen years for murder. He was terminally ill. He died five days after tasting freedom.

"What do you think about Moochie's chances?" Tracy asked before I headed to the hearing. "What if he isn't paroled. How would you feel?"

I didn't answer but knew I wanted Moochie free as much for Mama as for him or me, even knowing the last time I saw Moochie, he was a crazy man locked away in solitary. On a lonely five-hour drive to McCormick Correctional, I thought about all the years we missed jogging together and laughing together. I thought about all the times my brothers and sisters would be piled into a brown, wood-paneled station wagon and be driven up and down the back roads of South Carolina seemingly every weekend when we were young to visit Moochie in whichever prison he had been transferred to. I began to think about the stack of letters he had written me, unopened in a Nike sneaker box in my room, and why I hadn't written him in return.

I arrived at the prison a couple of hours early. It was, like all the others, too large, too ugly, in the middle of nowhere South Carolina, surrounded by a tall fence topped with barbed wire and backed by another tall fence. It was made of red brick. Supply trucks and small buses were entering and exiting a separate gate and being searched, including by a guard running a mirror on wheels beneath each vehicle in the way I'd see security officials do in movies involving the White House or the United Nations building in New York.

I paced back and forth, walking repeatedly from my Saturn to the long line of people forming outside the glass-encased visitor processing area. There were times we visited Moochie during heavy rainstorms and in icy conditions and were made to stand in single-file lines outside trying to not get wet or too cold until the guards decided to let us inside. That day the weather was mild, probably in the low nineties, and not particularly humid for a late summer day in steamy South Carolina. I stopped pacing when Mama, Willie and his fiancée, two preachers, Aunt Doretha, and a lawyer arrived. I was glad to see them. I didn't want to face the parole board alone, me and my stutter potentially the only things standing between Moochie and freedom.

But I would have.

"Nineteen years is long enough," Willie said to everyone and no one.

We walked in through a wire mesh door, down a long concrete walkway surrounded by tall fences and barbed wire, and through a brown metal door where we were met by another prison guard, who checked our identification. It's possible I'm mixing up the details about the look of the prison. After years of visits, it became nearly impossible to tell them apart.

Only five of us would be allowed in, the guard told us.

"Choose the best speakers," she counseled.

Mama, Willie, Moochie's lawyer, and Bishop Gibbs, the pastor of St. Stephen Holiness Church when I was a young boy, were chosen. So was I. We filed into the visiting room. It was large, drab, full of people waiting to see their sons, husbands, brothers. A single-file line of eight female prisoners, each of them black, was led in to await their turn before the parole board. Then we saw Moochie, all six feet, two inches of him. He wore a bright yellow jumpsuit. Shackles once again adorned his ankles, while handcuffs and chains dangled from his wrists and waist.

None of it dulled the smile beaming from his face. He called to us as a guard unlocked his chains and placed him in a closet-sized holding room just on the other side of one of the visiting room doors, close enough for us to see him through the bars in the cell door. He was bounding up and down, up, then down, like a prize horse ready to break free from the Kentucky Derby starting gate. Mama smiled back; Willie did, too, while noting how thin Moochie had gotten. We waved and smiled as Moochie peeked his head through the bars. No one mentioned the intra-family debate we'd had for years. Should Moochie hold fast to his faith and keep his dreadlocks? Or should he cut them and conform to adhere to SCDC policy?

I smiled but didn't know how to react to Moochie's excitement. I looked at him, though found myself involuntarily looking away, not knowing what to think, afraid to join in too furiously with his joy, though afraid not to. I wanted to be sure he'd be leaving with us that day, or at least begin an exit procedure that could lead him to us by the end of the year. That's what the *possibility* of parole can do to families, force you to prepare for something over which you have little control, make you grateful for the chance and dread it nevertheless, like hoping the lottery will free you from poverty.

After Moochie was placed in his cell and the door was closed, removing him from our view, we sat at a table for two hours thinking of reasons it was going to be his day to taste freedom. Willie and I eventually dozed off. I think Mama did, too.

"He's up next," a guard called.

For the first time, my nerves kicked in. It was a false alarm, though. The board was running behind. For another thirty minutes, we aimlessly, wordlessly milled around the visiting room.

The guard readied us again. "Okay, it's his turn."

Moochie was led to the other side of the waiting room. We followed and hugged him, giving him encouragement. He smiled as though he was already free. We smiled along with him.

"Man, I'm ready," he said. "I'm ready. I'm gonna let them know what I learned."

We told him that was a bad idea, because we all knew what he meant about what he had learned, about the connection between Africa and American slavery and the predicament of many of the black men who were behind bars with him and the factors that led them to prison. He had read so many books he wanted to drop knowledge on the parole board about white racism and black strength.

He wanted to drop that knowledge on everyone, and the board would be just another captive audience. He had become so insistent, it was all he could think about and all he could write about in letters to us. That's one of the reasons I stopped reading them. It had become a turnoff to even his family; no doubt it would have gone badly with the parole board.

"Calm down, Moochie, calm down," Willie said. "Gotta stay focused on today, just trying to get out. Africa can wait."

Moochie listened intently, silently, as Mama and Willie told him we needed him home to help get Zadoc and James back on track, that we all wanted him home. Willie and I stood before our oldest brother and reminded him the parole board needed to know the man sentenced two decades earlier was gone, that the man sitting before them was mature and bright, and loving.

Convince them, we urged, that he was more than the murder he confessed to committing.

We were led into a small room with a large TV and a table and three plastic seats lined up on the back wall. Moochie sat between his lawyer and Mama at the table, Willie, Pastor Gibbs, and me in the chairs behind them. I quietly wondered if I should speak, afraid my tangled tongue wouldn't let me.

"This hearing is for Mtume Obalaji Mfume, serving a life sentence for murder," a voice from the TV rang out. "Anybody here to speak on his behalf can begin."

We didn't know the Bunch family had already given their take.

"Moochie is a changed man," his lawyer began. "He feels extreme remorse about the night in question. His dreadlocks, in fact, are a sign of his deep faith and signify a positive, powerful change in his life."

The lawyer had pages of prepared text but the voice from the TV cut him off, said it wanted to hear from family members. Willie told the board about how Moochie found time to help him with his basketball skills the day Moochie was allowed to attend Daddy's funeral.

"For weeks, coaches had been working with me, but I just couldn't get it right. And Moochie, in that little bit of time, showed me what was wrong, and I got it. I can't tell you how many times and how many things and in how many ways Moochie taught us." Willie's words were smooth, as though he was giving a Ted Talk.

"Without him there teaching us, man," Willie continued, "we couldn't have grown into the men we are today. We need our brother. We have two younger brothers right now who need that same guidance, that same strong presence that only Moochie can provide for this family. Man, I have so much to say..."

"Seems like you don't need him that much; you turned out pretty well without him," the voice from the TV screen returned.

Such is the life of a convicted murderer's brother. Your success proves, in the judgmental eyes of outsiders, your brother could have overcome like you did, if only he had made wiser choices. Had you failed, that would be laid at his feet because he was a bad influence.

"Does his other brother want to say something?" the voice from the TV screen said.

"My name is Issac Bailey, and Moochie left us when I was about nine years old," I began, spitting words from my mouth faster than I had in years. "And I can tell you that, um, ah, um, ah, um, um, um, ah, um, um, ah, ah, um, um, um, that even though he has, um, ah, ah, um, ah, um, ah, um, ah, um, um, ah, been in here, um, ah, um, ah, um, ah, um, ah, he has been um, ah, um, ah, um, teaching me."

Moochie's lawyer turned unsteadily toward me, his head slowly swiveling on his neck, his torso stationary, the diameter of his eyes expanding.

Get with it! I know he wanted to yell because I saw a similar expression on Pastor Gibbs's face. Willie and Mama sat stoically as I spoke, not taking their eyes off the screen. I don't remember the parole board's facial expressions, likely because I did what I often did during horrible speech blocks, fix my gaze on a ceiling tile or spot high on a wall.

"Um, ah, and, um, and, um, ah, um, he has taught me that by, um, ah, um, um, um, um, ah, um, ah, and, um, remaining so strong, and, um, and, um, while in this place. And, um, ah, um, um, ah, ah, um, ah, um, ah, um, ah, um, he has read more books, um, ah, and, um, ah, um, um, ah, ah, um, ah, than I have out here."

There I was, a professional journalist, a married man, a soon-to-be father, a graduate of a top-rated college, still too dumb to talk. Shame bubbled up from the bottom of my toes and enveloped my entire being. The thought of letting Moochie down became more vivid by the second, though nothing would have stopped me from continuing speaking had not the voice from the TV cut me off and asked to hear from Moochie.

"Sir," Moochie said. "I know that crime was a terrible thing, and I'm sorry for that, and will try everything I can to make up for it. Man, oohhh. I don't know that there are words to express my regret for what happened that night."

His voice was soft, halting, not booming the way it had been minutes before. He was stuttering the way fluent speakers stutter, carefully searching for the perfect word in the perfect sentence that never materialized in his brain.

"Man, I know that crime was... I've been studying in here, taking a lot of classes, and have learned a lot," Moochie continued. "I'm not that little boy who came in here nineteen years ago. Man, I'm ready. Oh, man, I'm ready."

His hands were folded in front of him on the table, feet close together, knees touching. He looked like a grade school student sitting in the principal's office. Did Daddy look like that each time he showed deference to every white person he met in a Jim Crow South that frowned upon black men acting like men? I wondered. Had we given Moochie bad advice? Maybe if the board could see his strength, his resolve, understand his deep intellect, it would have been better.

Moochie went on for a few minutes before Mama chimed in, said that everything at home was in place for him to make a successful reentry into society, that Moochie would be working and staying with her until he established himself independently. She spoke briefly about our younger brothers and the powerful impact Moochie's presence would have on them.

"We need him home," she said, still stoic, still staring at the screen.

"*I* need him home..." Her always clear, powerful voice trailing off.

"Thank you," the voice in the TV told us. "Y'all can leave now. We'll let you know in a few minutes."

An excited energy ushered us out of the room. While we waited, we rejoiced, could feel that our family was about to be put back together.

"Powerful!" Moochie said, pointing to Willie. Pastor Gibbs and Moochie's lawyer joined in on the praise. Mama told them not to forget about me. Everything was upbeat, the anticipation intoxicating. *Moochie's coming home! Moochie's coming home,* we all were thinking.

Pats on the backs were being dished out, hearty hugs shared. We passionately shook the hands of every guard near us, and maybe a few prisoners, too, like a delirious basketball coach whose team had just won a championship on a last-second shot and couldn't contain the joy pulsing through his veins.

"Your petition for parole has been denied." The prison official walked up to us, whispering the news.

Our joy dried up as quickly as it had rained down.

I wondered if I had been the wrong choice to speak before the board. Maybe Willie was, too, because he was successful and showed no signs of the ill effects of having his big brother away for so long. Maybe Zadoc and James and my youngest brother, Jordan, or Moochie's only son, Albert (Smooch), would have been better choices because of their struggles. Maybe if the parole board could have known what happens when a pillar of an already-vulnerable family is removed—the problems that too frequently sprout—they would have been moved enough to consider that two decades in prison was a harsh enough punishment, even for Moochie's horrific act. Piecing a fractured family back together could head off even more problems. Why can't that help justify the granting of parole?

Would the board have cared to know that the success of the oldest boys in the family—those who knew Moochie best, watched him be family protector and role model, then watched drugs and bad decisions turn him into a convicted murderer—had become a kind of barrier between us and our youngest brothers, boys who had grown to believe that *real* men were those who went to prison and survived, like Moochie, not those who had avoided it? Moochie would have a better chance of reaching them, and at maybe stopping another cycle of violence. Why would that matter to parole board members when it didn't matter in 1982? Such is the incongruity of the American criminal justice system; it purports to want not only to punish but to prevent crime, yet its remedies often make more crime likely. Men who murder must be made to face the consequences of their actions; injustice would prevail if they didn't. But not factoring in the impact that punishment has on their families, most of them contending with psychic scars and generations-deep challenges, almost guarantees future bad behavior.

We hugged Moochie one last time, then watched as two guards led him away to a SCDC van, back to his base prison.

"That's the first parole hearing I was in that didn't work," Pastor Gibbs said.

Willie and I quickly zeroed in on what we believed was the real problem: dreadlocks.

"How can he expect to get out when he's on lockup? There's no way until he follows their rules," Willie said. "I'm going to write him and write him and write him until he listens."

I drove away numb, but also vowed to badger Moochie to cut his hair. I wouldn't write that letter to Moochie, though. I was tired of banging my head against a rock, against Moochie's insistence that his hair wasn't to be touched, and against a system whose rigid rules meant Moochie's release was always going to be a long shot, dreads or closely cropped hair. I later met one of the parole board members. He had been following my work through *The Sun News*.

"If your brother doesn't cut his hair, it's going to be hard to let him out," he said.

Those dreadlocks may represent a deep spirituality to Moochie but were a sign of defiance to a system that needed assurances that Moochie really had changed, he told me.

I thanked him for his honesty and told Willie and Mama what he said. I then showed up for two more parole hearings over the next few years, both after Moochie had cut his hair and been allowed back in the general prison population and was again earning *good* time, though he also received at least one demerit. He had said something suggestive to a female guard and was made to wear a pink jumpsuit for a time.

I wouldn't attend any more hearings than those. I couldn't take it. I felt a little piece of me die each time we walked into one and out again without Moochie, especially when it was clear that in one of them he had left his crazy phase (the further away he got from solitary, the more Moochie-like he seemed), expressed remorse, and done everything we told him he must.

Each of the parole hearings I attended, and the half dozen I didn't, ended like the first, just like every attempt I made to reconcile with my stutter.

"Denied."

Bet Bailey

I heard the scream come from next door. The primal fear in that voice startled me, but not as much as what came next. I was still one of the youngest members of the family. Maybe it was shortly before Moochie had been taken away in 1982, or shortly after.

I saw Mama in a housecoat at the neighbor's, out back. I saw the screaming black woman, running away from her home as though chased by a ghost. Then I saw a little boy, maybe a year or two younger than I was. He was stark naked. His skin was caramel-colored like mine. His hair was nappy like mine. His legs and arms were as skinny as mine, his chest as underdeveloped. His house was wooden, nearly cabin-like and shabby—sunlight peaked through its roof and floor—and would be destroyed a few years later. Mine was a single-wide mobile home made of tin that would be damaged beyond repair in 1989 by Hurricane Hugo. I'm sure he was eligible for free lunch at school, like I was, and relied upon the federal summer lunch program for a significant portion of his nutritional needs.

When I saw the boy, I couldn't tell if he was running away from Mama or toward his mother until I saw two long, squirming worms protruding from his anus. If you didn't pay attention, you could have mistakenly believed he had two tails. I don't know if he was screaming, because his mother's screams would have drowned them out anyway. We weren't far removed from abject poverty, but we weren't poor like he and his mother were.

Mama ran faster than I thought she could and caught up to the little boy and grabbed the back of his left arm with her left hand. She bent down to reach his butt. With her right hand, covered by a piece of plastic, she grabbed the dangling worms, threw them on the ground, and let the boy, still naked, go. He ran behind his mother. I couldn't see if he caught up to her. That episode convinced me of two things: that as hard as we had it, we were still blessed in ways others around us weren't, and that Mama was tougher and more caring than I'd ever be.

★ ★ ★

"Ikey," Mama yelled to me.

"Ma'am?"

"Go check on your uncle Harry; see if he needs anything."

I think I was in high school when Mama gave me that command. I had reached the age at which the demands she had made of my older siblings were now mine. I walked out of our house, a double-wide manufactured home with a few hand-built rooms and porches, to where Uncle Harry stayed, about a hundred feet away in a former homemade carport that had been transformed into a small wooden apartment. I found him lying in his bed, sprawled out on his stomach on top of white sheets. He was wearing a white T-shirt and white boxer shorts that fit like an oversized potato sack on his thin, and thinning, frame. His skin was dark and leathery like my father's. A smile was stuck to his face even when he was in a drunken stupor. He wasn't drunk that day. He was dying.

"Uncle Harry, you need anything?" I almost whispered, not wanting to wake him, not because I knew he needed rest, but because I knew why Mama sent me to him. I was nervous, not sure I was up to the task.

He mumbled an incomprehensible reply like he often did. On days when he was up and about, he would laugh and laugh and laugh, and ask for a beer or "some change" and constantly and aggressively scratch his head and rub his stomach. I wouldn't learn until later he was likely self-medicating a mental illness with his drinking. I never thought to ask about it then, probably because I mistakenly thought of him as little more than my uneducated, wandering uncle.

"Ikey. Hey, Ikey, you got two dollars?" he'd say just about every time he saw me, at the house, or when he was milling around downtown St. Stephen in front of a convenience store.

"Thank you!" he'd giddily say when I said yes, but he didn't press when I said no.

He was my uncle, whom I loved because I knew my Mama loved him. She took care of him until he died, just as she had taken in the kids of one of her younger sisters who died too soon, as well as a couple of her brothers who struggled with alcohol and various ailments.

She had been the sacrificial lamb of her generation of the family.

"Bet took on a lot," my aunt Doretha said, referring to my mother, Elizabeth Bailey McDaniel, by her nickname. "She looked out for us."

While other siblings were able to escape St. Stephen and the South to make their way to places like Baltimore and New York, she was the pretty little girl given to an older man to marry. She was frequently left to deal with the ramifications of her father's drinking, as well as my father's drunkenness, verbally battling police officers who frequently jailed my grandfather and her husband, and upsetting social norms. It took a special kind of woman to be willing to stand up that way because in the South into which my parents and aunts and uncles were born, the terrorists were fellow Americans who lived among the terrorized and used the criminal justice system to terrorize them even further.

They knew white men with hoods and guns and fiery crosses and hate in their hearts were always lurking and that the American criminal justice system exploited black men as de facto slaves deep into the twentieth century. It's why between my father's birth early that century and mine in 1972, roughly six million black people—including my aunts and uncles who lived long enough—fled the South. They had reason to be fearful. The irony of twenty-first-century America is that white violence against black people—black people being literally burned alive as mobs of white people cheered on, black towns burned to the ground because they became too prosperous for white tastes, black women raped by white men at will—is one of the nation's most enduring legacies, and yet it is black men who have become the nation's boogeymen.

White violence against black people was routine and occurred throughout the country. Here is an account of a 1940 incident that happened seven miles from St. Stephen, as recounted in *Sundown Towns: A Hidden Dimension of American Racism* by James W. Loewen:

According to the Rev. [Robert] Mack, the bus developed motor trouble and was driven into a filling station at Bonneau and left by the driver with consent of the operator while another bus was being secured from North Charleston. Leaving Bonneau at 10 o'clock for the second bus, the driver returned at midnight.

As passengers were transferring to the second bus eight white men drove up and ordered the excursioners to "get out here right quick. We don't allow no d—n n—rs 'round here after sundown." The excursioners, the white driver, and the station operator tried to explain the emergency to no avail. A second car drove up with eight more white men who began firing on the group with shotguns. Having no weapons, the excursioners fled into nearby woods. Many were still missing when the bus left at one Monday morning.

Mama was born less than two years later. That's the woman who casually told me to check on her brother and knew—*knew*—I'd listen without her having to say another word.

I walked over to the edge of Uncle Harry's bed and touched the back of his left shoulder. He began turning over. Slowly. I helped him sit up. My chin just over his left shoulder and my left cheek on his, I put my arms under his and began lifting, as though I was doing a set of squats in the weight room for football. Somehow, in that pose we stumbled over to the toilet about a dozen feet away, squeezing into the tight bathroom. He leveraged himself on the sink with one hand while I pulled down his boxers. A long stream of blood-soaked urine exited him—more blood than urine—and left wet red splatters inside the toilet bowl and on the seat and floor and on his underwear. I was horrified by the blood. He said nothing, didn't flinch, as though numb.

I pulled up his boxers with one hand, steadied him with the other. We stumbled back to his bed. He quickly assumed the previous pose, alive but all but dead to the world. I left.

"Is your uncle Harry okay, Ikey?" Mama asked.

"Yes ma'am," I returned, not sure if I was lying or being truthful because I knew she knew his condition better than I did. She was making sure he got as much medical help as she could. Her command, to go to Uncle Harry, was more to help me than him.

"All God's creatures," she'd often say to me, "deserve to be loved. All means *all*."

★ ★ ★

By the time Mama was telling me to check on Uncle Harry, she had begun taking in a series of troubled young men as a foster mother while providing respite for older men (and some women) who were mentally challenged, addicted to alcohol and drugs or disabled and couldn't care consistently for themselves. She bought several plots of land in St. Stephen, putting trailer homes on them, providing a place for dozens of the town's downtrodden to lay their heads. She helped them manage the little money they generated doing odd but sporadic off-the-books jobs, and from governmental benefits, including from Veterans Affairs and the local welfare office.

Mama couldn't heal them of their demons—more than once did I leave college on a break only to be greeted by drunk, smiling men milling around Mama's house—but she made sure there was food in their refrigerators, shoes on their feet, clothes on their backs. It was jarring to exit the bubble that was Davidson and reenter a St. Stephen that was growing more foreign by the month. And my mother was in the middle of it, trying to hold back the tide of violent crime and poverty that was taking hold across the country, a tide that led to harsh criminal sentences that would further destabilize already-vulnerable communities.

At Davidson, I was praised for having overcome and making it to a world-class institution of higher learning, supposedly to prepare me to help create a better world. Back home, Mama, with a grade school education, was already busy doing that work, comforting the least of these the way the preachers at White Chapel Holiness Church told us Jesus commanded. She took on the toughest cases, the lepers of their day. I was overwhelmed by achieving the lowest score on a test in a class full of white students. And I was feeling put-upon when white Davidson students would whisper, and sometimes scream, that black students like me weren't qualified to be in their presence. That's as Mama was staring down the town sheriff and his deputies and judges to make sure even the most hardened criminal was treated with respect. I was complaining the college newspaper didn't have diverse voices and was called brave for adding mine. Mama was protecting the powerless from the powerful.

I was wondering if it would be too much to juggle football and stay on top of my Davidson academic workload and mentor young kids on the other side of the tracks. Mama was making it possible for poverty-stricken elderly in St. Stephen to get around town, trying to ensure they wouldn't live their final days in isolation. About 11 percent of households in St. Stephen are of residents at least sixty-five years old living alone.

Mama kept those she brought in as busy as possible, had them planting watermelon and corn and butter beans in a small garden, helping my stepfather take apart car engines and put them back together again, mowing yards, assisting with Sheetrock installation and roof repairs for various needy residents. That kept the number of fights among that distressed group to a minimum but could not prevent them all. Some became bloody encounters and made Mama's house a not-infrequent stop for EMS and police.

She took them to church, spoke up for them in court, urged those capable to get more education or marketable skills and made way for them to attain it. She ran for town council twice and lost but only barely, with much of her support coming from the town's demoralized and displaced, people who usually didn't vote but showed up at the voting precinct in wheelchairs or after walking a few miles just to cast a ballot for her.

She officially had thirteen children, eleven who made it into the world and two who died in her womb. Unofficially, she had dozens, including some her age and older, because of the responsibilities she decided to take on, responsibilities others seemed unwilling or incapable of fulfilling. Me and my brothers and cousins pitched in where we could, with those who remained in St. Stephen taking on a heavier load as the years grew long.

I broke up a couple of fights between a few drunk tenants who were known to beat on each other and sometimes use knives. My first serious car wreck came during my early twenties when I was on a break from Davidson. I was transporting two of Mama's tenants to a nearby town because they said they needed a ride, something Mama had asked me to do dozens of times. We were hit by a drunk driver. My blue Chevy Nova was totaled. My two passengers were transported to the hospital with minor injuries.

"Ikey, you should have asked me first," Mama gently scolded me. "I know how to read them better than you. When they ask for something, sometimes you gotta say no."

I never thought doing such things constituted a burden because Mama never talked of Uncle Harry, or any of the scores of people she helped, as burdens. Her example sent a clear message, that you provide the needy as much dignified assistance as possible, no matter the lives they had lived, no matter the crimes they committed or the mistakes they made.

That's why for years Mama's place served as a kind of homeless shelter and one-stop shop for the needy in St. Stephen. That was no small task in an area whose per capita annual income, about eleven thousand dollars, was one of the lowest in the nation while its rate of poverty was among the highest in the region. Roughly 40 percent of St. Stephen residents are considered poor, including about 56 percent of children. Not a few times tenants would agree to pay the modest fee she'd ask for rent or commit to a few hours of work to help around the house, or help others, then break that promise and try to stay in one of her trailers against her wishes. Often, Mama found ways to work around those shortcomings and help them anyway.

During all of that, she found time to earn her GED a little more than half a century after her chance at a formal education was stolen from her by Jim Crow and a forced early marriage. She was proud some of her kids had attained lofty educational and professional credentials, which is what she always dreamed. It had to eat at her some, knowing that had she been born at a different time under different circumstances, she, too, would have excelled academically. She couldn't repair the damage caused by a South that held in contempt those who wore skin the color of hers. Defying that system—proving she could not only succeed but help as many others as possible—drove her. Drives her.

That's why Mr. Bunch being killed by the hands of her oldest child rocked her like little before or since. In some ways, it meant she had failed in her quest to overcome all she had faced, that the *white man* had won again, even though it was a white man who was murdered. The *white man* set us on an awful course, stealing us from Africa and enslaving and raping and beating us, then lynching us, then putting us on the back of the bus and forcing us to raise their children, who treated our men and women like kids, then banning us from the best neighborhoods and schools, then blaming us for the resulting maladies.

But many black families found a way to navigate through it all without succumbing to prison and fulfilling a stereotype. I know Mama wanted us in that number. I know that because she couldn't make that happen—Moochie's imprisonment ended that dream—she wanted to make amends even though she had done nothing wrong. That's why she went to the scene of the crime in 1982, quietly praying while watching police rope off the area and collect evidence.

She continued along that path by attending Mr. Bunch's funeral and apologizing directly to his family. She's never admitted it, but I don't doubt that Moochie's imprisonment provided the motivation she needed to embrace everyone, no matter how much the broader society looked down upon them. Mr. Bunch's murder was brutal and wrong. Because he was taken by Mama's oldest child, that guaranteed she'd spend the rest of her life trying to save others.

It also guaranteed the environment my youngest brothers grew up in was nothing like the one me and my older siblings experienced.

North Charleston's Most Wanted

I was walking from class to my dorm when it happened: someone offered me illegal drugs for the first time. I was a sophomore at Davidson College. How I had made it out of St. Stephen without once being tempted with drugs remains one of the great mysteries of my life. I grew up during the height of a drug and violence crisis that destroyed not only urban communities in large cities, but small, rural, Southern neighborhoods like mine. A childhood friend is blind today because of a bullet to his brain after a fight at a nightclub when we were in high school. My father abused alcohol. My oldest brother was high while killing a man. And yet, I never touched the stuff.

That's why I know an outsized courage and moral clarity were not why I successfully navigated situations that caused others to fail. I was as flawed as everyone else. In a very real sense, I succeeded because no one forced me—or even invited me—to the dark side. I wonder, too, if the blinders I was wearing while grappling with stuttering blinded me to temptations others couldn't avoid. I never had to "just say no" because no one tried to get me to say yes.

"Ike," a student called to me. "We're going to do some now. Wanna join us?"

"Nah, I'm good," I said and kept walking.

He was wearing a faded red baseball cap and customized faded blue jeans designed to look worn. He was white, maybe half a foot shorter than me. He was eager to get wherever he was going on that Friday afternoon. He mentioned cocaine or marijuana, maybe both, the drugs my youngest brothers had begun dealing in St. Stephen by that point, destroying their own lives and negatively affecting many others in our small town.

Drug abuse hadn't destroyed that white Davidson student's life. He was attending one of the nation's most exclusive colleges and eventually left with a prestigious degree that meant he was more likely to end up wearing five-hundred-dollar shoes on Wall Street than encounter prison bars. He spoke about using drugs with an anticipatory giddiness young men usually reserve for a first date with a girl they have long pursued. He was so excited he shared the news with me, someone he barely knew. He wasn't quite shouting, but wasn't whispering as we walked past other students.

He seemed shocked I would turn him down. He didn't know what I knew or what I had seen, including a small plastic bag of colorful drugs Moochie had hidden in our house when I was a boy. He didn't know Moochie was high and drunk when he stabbed Mr. Bunch to death.

He didn't know I was afraid drugs and alcohol might awaken in me what they may have awakened in my grandfather, father, and oldest brother. He didn't know I was afraid I, too, was secretly a violent man who would follow in their footsteps if I wasn't hyperaware about what I was doing and with whom and where. Drugs were recreation to him, death and destruction to me.

★ ★ ★

About the time my niece's mother was being killed in a drive-by shooting in an apartment she shared with my brother Jordan, a man named Henry P. Bennett Jr. from Huger, a small unincorporated area a few towns away from St. Stephen (formerly home of a slave plantation called Blessing), was being convicted and sentenced to life in federal prison for cocaine trafficking. Nearly a decade later, during the final full day of President Obama's second term, Bennett would become one of a record number of federal prisoners to receive a reduced sentence during a single presidency. Obama did it to begin righting the wrong that once was the hundred-to-one drug sentencing disparity between powder and crack cocaine (since reduced to eighteen-to-one) and other harsh war-on-drugs laws, which fueled a prison population explosion and the demise of too many black families during the 1980s and 1990s. Democrats and Republicans, white leaders and black leaders, were trying to curtail a crime rate that had been steadily climbing.

The Obama administration focused its mercy on nonviolent felons, particularly those serving time for drug-related crimes, a tactic embraced and touted by many activists urging criminal justice and prison reform. Violent felons are considered too big a risk for such mercy. In the minds of many, it is hard to justify allowing a man to go free when the person he harmed is dead forever and his family can never hug him again.

Bennett had not been convicted of killing anyone. Neither had Troy Gilmore, of Eutawville; Burnette Trione Shackleford of Georgetown; Moses King of North Charleston; or Deon Christopher Nowell of Charleston, other prisoners who had lived within a short drive of St. Stephen when they were convicted for a variety of drug-related offenses. Each had his sentence shortened along with Bennett's.

"Stories of rehabilitation and growth, of families reunited, and lives turned around—these are the stories that demonstrate why our nation is a nation of second chances," Neil Eggleston, Obama's White House counsel, said in a statement about the commutations.

Bennett was among fifteen South Carolinians in the final round of Obama commutations. His life sentence was reduced to one that should last a little more than twenty-two years, about ten years shorter than the time Moochie spent behind bars for killing Mr. Bunch.

★ ★ ★

"My name, um, my name, um, um, um, um, um is I-I-I-I-Is-Issac Bailey," I told the judge. "My um, brothers, um, um, um, um, um, um can stay with me in um, um, um, um, Myrtle Beach."

I was standing in the Berkeley County Courthouse speaking to a judge who resembled the local TV news anchor in 1982 who reported Moochie was facing murder charges and potentially the death penalty. She was a blond in a black robe sitting on high while peppering me with questions. Tracy and I hadn't been married long but had moved into a cozy three-bedroom, two-bathroom house, I managed to sputter to the judge.

Zadoc and James were standing quietly. They had gotten arrested again. I had long lost count of how many times. I showed up at their bond hearing to support Mama emotionally but ended up telling the judge my brothers could move in with me, that it would be good to get them out of St. Stephen. I didn't tell her I had gotten them out of St. Stephen a few years earlier, taking them to Davidson. I didn't tell the judge I wasn't sure it would be fair to my new wife to take these two young men, with their long criminal records, into our new home, didn't tell her that I had begun losing faith in their ability, or desire, to change.

I had grown frustrated and convinced the streets of St. Stephen were safer when my brothers were behind bars, that our family knew that during those periods we wouldn't get a 3:00 a.m. phone call telling us my brothers had either killed or been killed during a drug sale gone wrong. I did not share those thoughts with the judge.

I seriously wondered if the ninety-minute drive between St. Stephen and Myrtle Beach was a long-enough distance to protect us from lingering ripple effects from bad acts Zadoc and James had committed, but I dared not reveal that concern to Mama, the judge, or Tracy. They were my brothers and I had a responsibility to help, I reasoned.

"Yes," I answered when the judge asked again if I was ready to take on the responsibility.

I would see her months later in a courtroom near Myrtle Beach when she took on temporary duty in Horry County during a judge shortage. I was covering a criminal trial for *The Sun News*. I sat in the back of the courtroom. I didn't tell her what happened after she allowed Zadoc and James to come home with me. Their stay lasted a week.

Tracy spent most of those days teaching high school English. I worked full days at *The Sun News*. Zadoc and James mostly sat in the house and milled around until we got home. Almost every night, I took them to Christ Community Church, a mostly white evangelical church where I was attending men's meetings and leading small race relations groups and studying the Bible while Zadoc and James sat in the lobby. By the end of the week, I had plans to take them to businesses with help wanted signs in their windows. Their securing jobs would have been something positive to tell the judge. We never made our job-hunting trip.

"Man, you treat us like kids up in this joint," James said. "We ain't kids."

"That's how you feel, too, Zadoc?" I asked.

Zadoc nodded his head yes.

"Fine. Let's go," I yelled.

"I'm taking them back right now! Right now!" I told Tracy.

We didn't speak a word in the car during the drive back to St. Stephen.

"You need to call the judge and tell her to revoke their bond and put them back in jail!" I told Mama. "They don't want to listen to anybody. They think they're men. Cool. Then let them be men and fend for themselves."

I knew, and so did Mama, that the arrangement we made with the judge had been a Band-Aid that couldn't hold. Her attempts at getting through to her youngest sons hadn't held. Willie's attempts didn't hold. Neither did Mel's or Jody's or Sherrie's, each of whom also took my younger brothers into their homes and away from St. Stephen or provided them opportunities to leave the drug game. The example of my stepfather, a man who provided a strong black role model and worked hard and taught his kids various craft skills, hadn't been enough to convince Zadoc and James to walk a different path.

I was relieved. I was ridding myself of a burden I didn't want to bear. I didn't know what to do and was tired of pretending I did. I had given up on them long before that week, believed whatever consequences were to come they would have earned. That's why I didn't fight harder to keep them in Myrtle Beach. That lack of fight likely saved my marriage; I was sure Tracy hadn't been comfortable with two strange young men with sketchy records in her new home and wasn't sure how much longer she could stand the arrangement. I didn't know if it would doom Zadoc and James.

Disappointment dripped from Mama's cheeks as I angrily explained why she needed to call the court and have Zadoc and James returned to lockup. She didn't resist me. It would be many years before she told me why.

★ ★ ★

"You don't know the half of what we did and got away with," James told me from the comfort of a prison in Bishopville.

James was about five years into a sixteen-year prison sentence linked to an attempted armed robbery of a drug dealer. Smooch, Moochie's only son, was serving a twenty-five-year sentence for his involvement in that crime, which left one of their accomplices dead, apparently from an inadvertent bullet from a gun Smooch was carrying. James was convicted as an accessory. He never entered the house, only drove Smooch and a younger man to the drug dealer's house and picked him up afterwards. I thought I knew but didn't fully grasp the extent and depth of the trouble my youngest brothers had been getting into. Had I known, I'm not sure I would have allowed them into my home with my new wife.

My youngest siblings and I grew up in the same house but vastly different environments. My role models were Doug, Willie, and Sherrie, who had made it into major colleges or begun raising families of their own and started careers. I wanted to be as good as they were. But each of us had left our childhood home by the time James and Zadoc were beginning to develop an acute awareness of the wider world; outside influences were bigger factors in their lives than ours.

My stepfather provided stability for my youngest brothers. They didn't have to cope with watching Daddy beat Mama like the rest of us did. But I didn't have to deal with growing up around the strange drunks, drug addicts, and drug dealers Mama was trying to save. She told me she knows that complicated things and would do some things differently had she another chance, but she doesn't regret helping so many people. James was being reared in that environment. His entrance into the world was the most unique of all. He was a developing fetus when Mama's body was absorbing the news her oldest son had killed a man and could be killed himself in South Carolina's death chamber. He had the darkest skin of any of us and felt the sting of that reality like most dark-skinned black Americans do, even within their own families or in their neighborhoods.

James was barely beyond his toddler years when alcohol and drug-addicted men would begin bribing him with a few dollars to sneak them an extra beer or bottle of wine or pack of cigarettes from the "store" Mama kept stocked in one of the rooms built onto our house, which also served as a recreation center, akin to the kind of store Mr. Bunch had owned in Bonneau. That room became a hangout of sorts for the young and old, another way to pay the family's bills, and an extension of Mama's entrepreneurial spirit. For James, it fueled what he said was a love of money and marijuana.

"When they used to hang out playing pool all day in the shop, what do you think they were doing while they were gambling on pool? Selling drugs and more," James said. "Moms and Pops didn't know nothing about that 'cuz they were trying to provide for the kids. I grew up around the biggest hustlers. I could have made different choices. I can't get around that. But I guess once I got to a certain level, there was no turning back."

While I was adjusting to life at Davidson College, in a world in which I rubbed elbows with the children of the wealthy and powerful, like a son of Strom Thurmond—a former segregationist who secretly fathered a black child while becoming one of the longest-serving U.S. senators ever—and learning from some of the country's top professors, James had already become a minor drug dealer known for an unrelenting, fearless attitude.

"My first serious crime was stealing Moms's pearl-handle twenty-two," he said. "Zadoc got the Maxima and we went to a football game at Timberland High School. After the game, we're leaving, we're pulling out from the high school, and I started shooting in the air. When we got to town, crossing the tracks, a Berkeley County cop came out of nowhere and put his lights on. I was around fourteen or fifteen at the time. Long story short, they searched the car and found the gun and called Moms."

Because of all the community outreach she was doing, and because she was the mother of "The Bailey Boys"—then a high compliment because her oldest children, after Moochie, had done so well academically and athletically—the cops took the gun from James, gave it to Mama, and let them go.

"But boy did I get my ass whooped!" James said.

The close call and second chance he received because of Mama's good reputation didn't deter James. Not much later, he watched as a man pulled up to a Fast Point in the middle of town, jumped out of his car, music blaring loudly from the speakers with the engine running, and walked inside the convenience store.

"I jumped in the car and joyride through Charleston that night," he said. "After that, park the car in a cut and strip it down for the twelve-inch rims and a turtleback punch amp. At the time, I was too young to know the motor was worth money, so I set the car on fire."

Before his life of crime took flight, someone noticed and tried to step in. Sherrie caught James and Zadoc smoking a "Philly blunt" given to them by Smooch. She scolded them, warned them of the dangers. James was in the fifth grade.

"After that, anytime something would happen, family and Moms would blame it on drugs and send me to Charter and other rehab centers like I was on crack or something," he said. "I was the only kid in rehab centers that never did coke, crack, and hard drugs. As time went by, I loved blowing green, and only thing it did was give me the munchies, besides mind stimulation."

He began selling "green," marijuana, to support his habit and to keep up with the lifestyles he saw a few other drug dealers in town living. That's when he got introduced to guns, mostly getting them from crack addicts and "white boys."

The *white boys* stole guns from a store in Bonneau and sometimes from a train stop near Charleston, where they'd find assault rifles on train cars from the nearby military base.

"White boys come through with guns you never seen before," James said. "They get them from the government and dump them in the hood so we could kill each other."

Fellow *black boys* had the same focus, just different targets. They would break into the homes of white people and single out off-duty police cars, searching for guns. Gun advocates argue that a gun in a home will scare away potential intruders. In the world in which my youngest brothers operated, the opposite was true. They flocked to the sites of guns.

Some of them swapped those stolen guns—and stolen jewelry and other stolen goods—for the drugs James was selling. He quickly made a name for himself, becoming a kind of legend on the streets and a pariah in the eyes of St. Stephen police.

By that time, it had become clear to Mama that a warning a psychiatrist made about James while he was in middle school had become reality. Like she had done with Moochie, Mama had taken James and Zadoc to a series of counselors and psychiatrists, hoping the right plan of treatment or the right pill—Zoloft, Ritalin—would help her steer them in another direction.

"Ma'am, if you don't get that young man out of your house and get him some real help, there is going to be a lot of trouble later," he told Mama.

During that period, another debate arose in our family about why our youngest members chose to follow in Moochie's footsteps. Was it because Mama had gotten too soft in her old age? She was blamed for having "spared the rod." The oldest among us were beaten with switches (small tree branches), leather belts, and electrical cords, anything she could find, hoping to beat us straight. That was not unique to our family or Mama. It's the way so many black parents had desperately done it with their kids before and after her. Many of us perversely credited those beatings for keeping us on the straight and narrow. But Mama's thinking on parenting evolved, from one predicated upon brute force to emphasizing active listening and compassion.

My youngest brothers also got their "ass beat," as James said, but not as frequently or fiercely. When my youngest siblings stepped out of line, Mama was more likely to reach for the phone book to call a counselor than a drop cord or switch. And she adopted a nonnegotiable philosophy, to never—ever—abandon a young person who had gone astray.

She was willing to try tough love. It took her years of emotional struggle, but she finally kicked James out of the house after one too many arrests. That was no small decision for a woman who didn't even want to evict drunk and drug-addicted strangers who refused to pay monthly rent. Mama wanted the move to be a wake-up call for James. He didn't take it that way.

"Once I got kicked out for my actions, I had to make ends meet," James said. "Either I eat or starve. And I wasn't going to starve."

★ ★ ★

Sitting at my desk in the *Sun News* newsroom, I was scrolling through pages of links on the internet doing research for a column when I happened upon "North Charleston's Most Wanted," a local list of fugitives police were most eager to find, patterned after "America's Most Wanted."

James and Zadoc made the list.

My heart sank when I saw their names. I wanted to melt

into the chair. My face burned hot with shame. Even though by that point I had been open about my family's struggles, I wanted to hide in a corner. I avoided eye contact and small talk with my colleagues. I had long dreaded the potential out-of-the-blue phone call delivering bad news about my youngest brothers; I didn't know I'd instead stumble upon it in the middle of the newsroom.

That sting didn't last long, because things got worse a short while later when I was forced to return to the Berkeley County Courthouse, where years earlier I had spoken on behalf of James and Zadoc. I sat in the final row of the room quietly listening to testimony. James was sitting in the defendant's chair next to his attorney. During the overnight break in the trial, we visited James in his holding cell and listened as he explained why he was convinced the jury would find him not guilty. That's why he was ignoring every plea offer from the prosecution.

"They ain't got no evidence on me, bruh," he said confidently. "No evidence."

I was flabbergasted. I sat through the trial and knew it was darn near impossible he wouldn't be found guilty. Smooch, who had begun serving his twenty-five-year sentence for his role in the crime, took the stand and explained what happened.

Smooch and a friend decided they had identified a "sweet lick," or caught a drug dealer in a vulnerable position, making him easy prey; they knew drug dealers were unlikely to go to the police to report that they had been attacked. They would go to the dealer's house, pretend to want to commence a drug interaction, and rob him—a tactic once used against James that almost resulted in his murder. Something went wrong while they were in the house and the gun Smooch was carrying went off and killed his partner.

James knew Smooch and his friend were going to commit the crime and agreed to take them to the drug dealer's house and pick them up afterwards. Upon hearing that, I texted Tracy that it was an open-and-shut case. There was a young black dude on the witness stand telling an all-white jury the role he and his black cousin played in a crime that ended in a man's death. Even if James had actually been innocent, the odds were good that he would be convicted.

I had sat in on several cases in several courtrooms as a journalist and was never more certain that there would be a guilty verdict, and yet James was equally certain he'd soon be going home. The same blood was running through our veins, but we were inhabiting different planets that day. The same was true of so many other days, when James said he led police on high-speed chases; when a gaggle of police officers—from several agencies, including K-9 units and helicopters—surrounded James and Zadoc at the park across from Mama's house; when disputes over drugs led rival groups to shoot up the trailer James and Zadoc had transformed into a "booming weed spot"; when our oldest cousin, Thomas, called the police because James and Zadoc had brought so much trouble near where he lived and he feared for his family's safety; when James wrestled a gun away from two intruders—childhood friends—who tried to rob him, sparking unrest in St. Stephen and surrounding towns as their feud grew in intensity.

"They thought I was going to give them the weed and money so easily. Wrong!" James said. "Long story short, I didn't give up a dollar—or a bag of weed."

But it wasn't just bags of weed. Cocaine became a product of choice as well because, as James claimed, "cocaine money is crazy."

"A kilo of cocaine and you could make over a hundred twenty thousand dollars," he told me.

It wasn't just the money. It was the rush. The high I got from scoring a touchdown on the football field, that's the kind of high he got when he committed crimes, James said. There was a perverse pride in what he was doing.

"Man, every time I walked away alive, the rush!" he said.

How did he score the cocaine, which turned an early marijuana habit into a game of cat and mouse with his life, and the lives of others in his orbit? The drug trafficking operation for which Henry Bennett—the man whose sentence was reduced by President Obama—was convicted and sentenced to life was said to have tentacles in multiple states. His reach skipped neither my youngest brother nor St. Stephen.

Bennett was eligible for commutation because he was a nonviolent felon. That doesn't mean he didn't leave a trail of violence in his wake; neither does it mean his sentence shouldn't have been shortened. (James agreed with the commutation.) We can't repair the damage done by mass incarceration by focusing solely on sympathetic cases. Men like my youngest brothers have caused great harm. We must reckon with how to better handle them, too.

The End in the Beginning

Jordan was in the perfect defensive crouch. It was a fall Friday night in the heart of the South, where football is like a religion. He was staring down a receiver named A. J. Green, holding his own even as Green made spectacular one-handed catches in the rain.

There he was, my youngest brother, defending the state's top receiver and eventual NFL All-Pro. Jordan was a linebacker, big enough to bother Green physically, fast enough to contend with Green's speed, a combination of athletic gifts that should have taken him further in football than my four-year career at Davidson. Instead, a few years after that game, Jordan and I were stepping over a bloody footprint greeting us at the door of his girlfriend's apartment. I couldn't tell if it was made by a cop's boot, an EMS worker's shoe, or a bare foot. It left an indelible spot on the concrete walkway just outside her front door.

"Get your stuff and don't ever come back!" a white woman was yelling at us from an apartment building away, her words shaking me free from an involuntary stare at the footprint. Jordan would later tell me she was the complex's manager.

Inside, a bloody white T-shirt was curled up in a corner of the small kitchen. Clothes were scattered throughout, on the floor, on the couch, on the bed, on the back of a couple of chairs. Crumpled papers were scattered about. A big-back color TV was sitting off-center of the small brown wood table struggling to hold it, as though someone knocked into it while rushing by.

Dime-sized holes, four, maybe five of them, were dotting a yellowing wall a couple of feet from a bunk bed where three kids younger than five years old had been sleeping while bullets were whizzing by a few hours earlier. The stuffed animals in the room were undisturbed.

I hadn't seen holes shaped that way since they were embedded in my parents' two-tone blue Chevy Blazer, which was sitting under a white tarp in our front yard like a body on a slab in a morgue. Those bullets and those holes—courtesy of a drive-by shooting I didn't find out about until weeks later because such things had become so routine it was hard for the family hotline to keep up with all the breaking news—provided enough reason to monitor my kids closely anytime we visited St. Stephen, which essentially felt like protecting them from my own mother. She would never hurt them, but neither could she shield them from an errant bullet. It was one of the most painful things I've ever had to do.

I desperately wanted Kyle and Lyric to spend lots of time with Mama, and I knew she desperately wanted to play a critical role in their lives. She has two dozen grandchildren, living in various parts of the country. Kyle and Lyric were a ninety-minute ride away but didn't see Mama much during my kids' early years. I feared they wouldn't be safe during visits to Grandma's because Mama's youngest children—Zadoc, James, Jordan—had become real-life menaces to society. The drive-by shooting that killed Jordan's girlfriend was the latest chapter of an ongoing dispute between a couple of my brothers and rivals who also sold drugs. In another incident, one of my brothers was chased off the road by a rival shooting at him—while two of my young nephews were in the truck.

My brothers wouldn't purposefully hurt anyone in our family. Still, their lifestyles endangered us anyway. I would only let my kids stay at Mama's house for hours at a time, never overnight, and only if I was around. I didn't know what else to do. I had to protect my kids. I had to honor Mama. That's why I was standing in Jordan's apartment staring at a bloody footprint, to support Mama, not Jordan, even though Jordan had just survived an assassination attempt.

When Mel, my youngest sister, called to tell me about the shooting, I was in Myrtle Beach teaching about criminal justice and race relations and trying to convince young black men to resist easy money and the dangers that came with it, yet feeling helpless I couldn't stop my brothers from being a terror in the streets of my hometown. Mama's house felt safe enough for the kids only when my youngest brothers were in jail or prison.

My youngest brothers had never been my heroes the way Moochie had been, and I'm not sure I've ever been theirs. It's as though we grew up in different worlds, even though we were nurtured in the same womb, in the same house, in the same town, in the same state, educated by the same public school system, and ate the same collard greens seasoned with ham hocks.

In so many ways, when I was stepping over that bloody footprint with Jordan, I was effectively standing next to a stranger. It was my first time in that apartment. I hadn't known that's where he occasionally lived. I knew Kim, his girlfriend, because our families have known each other for years, but I didn't know her well, didn't know she and Jordan had been dating until they produced a little girl together, one of the handful of kids asleep in their beds when bullets began ringing out from guns being held by a couple of guys who snuck into the parking lot under the cover of dark. They ducked under the bedroom window and repeatedly fired, trying to hit Jordan but not realizing, or caring, that the mother of his daughter was sleeping next to him on the bed and a few toddlers were asleep in another room.

The guys, we were told, had first driven around town looking for Jordan at Mama's house before making their way to his apartment. I wanted to lash out at Jordan. To put himself in harm's way was awful enough. To make Mama a potential victim because of his choices, I didn't have the words to describe my rage, my sense of helplessness.

"Don't you ever come back! Don't you ever come back here, god damn it!" The woman was still yelling as Jordan and I picked up a few of his belongings, shirts and pants and underwear, boom box, DVD player, and placed much of it in plastic bags. Hand signals and small nods of the head were all the communication we could muster as we walked through the handful of rooms in the redbrick apartment, pointing to items that needed to be packed and those that could be left behind. There wasn't much to say.

"I don't ever wanna see you around here again! Ever!" the woman kept screaming as we walked back to my truck.

Moochie's imprisonment had hung over the family like a dark cloud, an ever-present storm even on sunny days. It brought a forever sadness. We weren't sad for our youngest brothers in the same way. We were baffled. And horrified. They hadn't witnessed Daddy's fists hitting Mama's flesh. They hadn't seen all the weekends Daddy came home drunk, or stayed out drunk, or felt the wrong end of his leather belt. We weren't rich when they were growing up, but we weren't nearly as poor as when the oldest among us were making our way through school. We emphasized education—in word and deed—and right-decision-making.

We provided good role models, older brothers who had gone on to success in college or work and marriage directly after high school. We had set a track record that could benefit them in school. Teachers expected big things from the Baileys and were willing to provide second chances and extra tutoring and guidance to tease out the abilities they knew each of us had. We had a stepfather who showed us how to work, and hard, how to build marketable skills that could be used just about anywhere even if college wasn't a good fit. And my youngest brothers didn't have to watch him beat Mama, because he never did, hardly ever raised his voice.

We had done all the things you hear psychiatrists and psychologists and street-corner preachers say you must in order to raise good, solid, responsible boys who would grow up to be good, responsible men. And yet, all I could think about while driving Jordan to Mama's house was the image of that bloody footprint, which embedded itself in my mind and wouldn't leave for months. And I was scared out of my wits that there soon would be more bullets, more death from an unending game of revenge drive-by shooting after revenge drive-by shooting. I can't remember if I said anything to Jordan until an hour later, telling him, in no uncertain terms, that we would be heading to the police, that he would tell them whatever he knew about why someone would try to kill him.

I wasn't thinking about the injustices in the criminal justice system, the ones I had been writing about in my column and uncovered during journalistic investigations. At that moment, I didn't care about questionable police tactics, wanted no part of lectures about young black men being railroaded or about the school-to-prison pipeline or talk of justice at all. Because Kim was dead. Because Jordan's decisions, something about his supposed role in the theft of an SUV and cocaine and his refusal to return the vehicle, contributed. Jordan didn't pull the trigger. He didn't kill Kim. But he had spent years making life dangerous for the mother of his daughter, and my mother. What happened was not unforeseeable.

This was pre–Trayvon Martin, Michael Brown, and Sandra Bland. There was no talk then of Black Lives Matter or Blue Lives Matter. This was long before a dispute would erupt over a painting by a high schooler from Ferguson—a police officer depicted as a wild boar, a protester as a wolf—in the Capitol building, long before *The Washington Post* and other news outlets would begin tracking police shootings because the federal government had not mandated such a thing. Freddie Gray's neck had yet to be broken. Tamir Rice wasn't yet a household name for having gotten shot by the police for playing with a toy gun in a park in an open carry state. It would be years before Donald Trump and his supporters would begin using "black on black" crime—the kind my youngest brothers were involved in, the kind that murdered Kim—to deflect debate about police brutality and misconduct.

Even if Kim's murder had happened in the middle of the national debate about police and crime and race, my reaction to Jordan would have been the same. I was that angry. I was that scared. I was that frustrated. I blamed Jordan's lifestyle choices for the bullet that had just snuffed out the life of my niece's mother. And I wondered what might have been. Why was he there? What was the difference between him and A. J. Green, the football player he matched up against so well in high school? Green was then at the University of Georgia breaking freshman receiving records, launching him into an otherworldly NFL career. He was honing his skills and God-given talents and putting them to good use. Why didn't Jordan? He was talented, too. He had role models, too, and opportunities, and plenty of people who cared about him and prayed with and for him and disciplined him and patted him on the back and took him into their homes to get him away from the mean streets of St. Stephen. And, still, there we were wondering what to do after his girlfriend was murdered.

Why couldn't the force of all his older brothers and two sisters and cousins who chose the military or built small businesses, and aunts and uncles who had come through some of the worst of what the mid-twentieth-century South had to offer, why did none of that get through to Jordan? What more could we have done? Why hadn't I done more? The questions sped through my brain, on a seemingly endless loop.

I felt myself wanting to cry. But I was all cried out. I had spent too many tears crying for Damon. I had spent too many tears crying in Mama's house, years before Kim's shooting, pleading with my younger brothers and oldest nephew, Smooch, to learn from Damon's example, to walk a different path before their fates merged. I thought they listened, thought they heard me when I told them all the reasons and ways Mama had been loving on them and why their decisions were making her life impossibly hard as she tried to support and love them while many of the rest of us had been warning her to let them suffer the consequences of their actions, believing it was the only way to wake them from their apparent stupor.

Every time we had that kind of talk, they always nodded their heads in agreement, saying they understood, that they needed to do better. And always we parted ways with a hug and a promise to stay in touch and my pledge that they could call for advice anytime. Every time we talked like that, it created the slightest bit of hope, the way

Moochie being eligible for parole always kept hope alive, no matter how many times his petition was denied.

But hope can be fleeting and isn't always motivating. No matter how many times we had those talks, no matter how many times we provided structure and guidance or took my youngest brothers into our own homes, they'd want to return to St. Stephen, where they kept getting arrested, kept getting deeper into a street drug game the rest of us never understood, kept opening themselves up to being killed or killing. I was thinking about all those things sitting in Mama's house with Jordan. I knew I didn't want to see another cycle of violence erupt in St. Stephen.

Maybe—just maybe—if the shooters could be identified and quickly captured, no more blood would be shed. I had no doubt that wouldn't be the last shooting. I didn't know the streets the way my youngest brothers did. I knew enough to know that such a thing hardly ever went unanswered, that it was biblical, an eye for an eye, a life for a life, that, to those involved, turning to the police would be taken as a betrayal of those principles. I'm not sure describing it as gang-related is accurate. For some reason, many young men in our town had crafted their own set of rules, rules only they fully understand, and my youngest brothers were in the middle of it all, risking imprisonment even as Moochie was pleading with the parole board to let him taste free air again.

The best I can determine is that it is akin to playing football. On the field, the rules are clear to the players and those who study the game closely but seem like Greek to outsiders. On the field, aggression and assault and physical and psychological and emotional dominance, the kind that would get you arrested or shunned in just about every other setting, are encouraged and rewarded. Hit the hardest, get a sticker on your helmet. Perform after sustaining a concussion or broken leg or after absorbing an ungodly hit, your standing increases. Jordan had the potential to be great on the football field. I didn't know he wanted to be great on the streets.

"Get up, Jordan," I said, jumping up from the couch. "Let's go. Right now!" I demanded, talking to him like a stern father, even knowing I would have had a hard time making him move had he resisted.

"Where you taking him?" Mama asked me.

"We are going to the police and he's going to tell them what he knows," I said, barely able to contain my anger. "He's gonna talk."

"Okay," Mama said in a voice that was part submissive, part relief. "The police said they wanted to talk to him anyway."

Jordan hopped in my truck without a fuss. He may have been dealing cocaine and carrying guns and getting into bloody fights on the streets. In our family, he was still just Jordan, the youngest, almost miracle child, born long after we thought Mama would have more kids, born a year or so after she had had her second miscarriage.

The police department was a five-minute drive away, on the other side of the tracks in St. Stephen. I took a detour to Moncks Corner, which meant driving by the cemetery where Mr. Bunch had been buried. I pulled into the driveway of a defense attorney who had handled criminal cases involving my family before. He said a quick consult would cost us fifty dollars. I paid.

I told him Kim died on the way to the hospital, that we believed the drive-by was really for Jordan, about my plan to take him to the police to talk.

"Anything we should be thinking about when we get there?" I asked.

He didn't say much. He did not offer to come with us. I left his office and headed directly to the police station, which was housed in a small trailer like the one we grew up in. Jordan and I walked inside. He sat in a chair in the lobby while I went to the front desk and told the receptionist who we were. A few minutes later, a detective came out to greet us.

"We'd like it if Jordan can come back and speak to us alone," he said, shaking my hand.

My instinct was to say no. I've counseled my own kids to never speak to the police without me or their mother. I ignored my instinct. I cared less about Jordan saying something incriminating than I did about trying to prevent more violence. I sat down and watched Jordan walk into a back room, where he and the detective were greeted by a couple of other officers. They shut the door behind them. I briefly thought about knocking on the door to force my way into the conversation. That thought was quickly replaced by the image of the bloody footprint.

I couldn't let go of the realization that someone else connected to my family had been murdered, couldn't stand the thought that more murder might come. No one in 1982 told us that nearly three decades later we'd be dealing with murder again. No one in 1982—not a counselor, not a victim's advocate, not a judge, not a lawyer, not a social worker—told us much of anything. Sitting in the waiting room of the police department, straining to overhear the raised voices of Jordan and the detectives, I had little doubt the shame we felt and didn't cope well with was partially responsible for Kim's death. That led to more shame. I didn't know if I had allowed fear and anger to force me into a rash decision, or if I had made the only responsible choice.

None of what I had learned through years of reporting and reflection and research about why cycles of violence in families occur—particularly when a breadwinner or role model is imprisoned—made that moment any clearer or easier. All I knew was that our family had been left behind by a system that did not care about us in 1982, a cycle of violence was in full bloom, and none of us knew how to stop it. Kim's death wouldn't be the last.

Real Men Go to Prison

It's hard to make out the images in the photo, taken with a contraband smartphone in a South Carolina prison. You can clearly see the blood; it covers the white clothes of a bearded inmate looking toward the camera. You can see the desperation in his eyes.

The blood is on the sheets behind him and other pieces of clothing (maybe T-shirts, maybe towels) and on white sheets of paper scattered across the floor. It—so much blood—is on the man over whom the bearded man is hovering while on his knees, as though pleading to a higher power to stuff life back into his friend's body. If so, his prayers didn't work. The man laid out on his back on a dark concrete floor in a small prison cell—decorated by a whiff of sunlight smuggling its way through a small window over a red cot on one wall and a metal door on another—either was dead by the time the picture was snapped by a fellow inmate, or certainly was when prison and emergency officials came to place his body in a black bag and haul it away.

A yellow-handled mop stood guard at the entrance of the cell. It had not yet been called into duty to clean up the blood. It looked like the industrial-strength mop I had used a thousand times at McDonald's when I worked in the grill area of the restaurant during high school. It's odd that seeing a mop in a photo of a minutes-old murder made me think about McDonald's instead of fully registering the horror of a man just robbed of his life. It happened in the prison and in the dorm where James was being held, meaning it could have just as easily been my brother, not a man I didn't know, lying in his own pool of blood. The photo was of a scene in Lee Correctional Institution, the largest prison in South Carolina, in the Chesterfield dorm, a place where I had visited Moochie multiple times while growing up.

That smuggled photo introduced me to that prison in a way I never had been. A man had been stabbed to death inside his small cell not too long before he was scheduled to be released. I was reintroduced to Lee because of a photo from a contraband camera phone taken by a prisoner who wanted to let the broader public know about life inside. The dead man in the photo had supposedly violated a gang code against the use of hard drugs, according to prisoners. He had been using something called "ice molly," and other such things that frequently got smuggled inside. The inmate, thirty-five-year-old convicted murderer Ae Kingratsaiphon, had barricaded himself in his room, maybe for hours, after getting high on the drugs and was denied food.

"They got tired of waiting on him to come out, so ten of them kept beating on the door until they got in the room," James told me.

The man who was killed was "a little Asian dude smaller than me, so about fifteen of them ran into the room and started stabbing him," James said. "Dude supposed to go home the next week. What's crazy is dude is from California and he can't even speak his family's original language. They stabbed him out of fear."

A shortage of prison guards throughout the state's correctional system meant the few on duty didn't always manage to make the rounds through the dorms on schedule. James said that was the case that day and why Kingratsaiphon's body lay on the floor in his cell alone for more than half an hour before anyone responded. They eventually took him out in a body bag and turned the scene over to SLED to investigate. The dead man's friend, who was kneeling over him in the photo, also suffered serious injuries and was taken to a nearby hospital. When the Charleston *Post and Courier* asked prison officials about the incident, this is how they responded:

"State Law Enforcement Division spokesman Thom Berry said the agency documented the scene for the Corrections Department. [A state official] said she could not release more details while SCDC police services is investigating the incident. The department refused to release an incident report from the event."

For the past few years, we've been debating, loudly and passionately, about the value of black life, or if black lives matter at all. That's mostly been about black people's interactions with police in high-profile cases of brutality and abuse and misconduct. That's mostly been about black people who are on the right side of prison walls and bars and fences, the ones still breathing free air. The debate about the other black lives—the ones overrepresented in an American prison system that holds 25 percent of the world's inmates even though the United States is home to only 5 percent of the world's population—has not had the same urgency. In a way, it's history repeating itself.

During the height of the antebellum era, free blacks faced discrimination in a thousand different ways. But they were free, at least ostensibly. Black slaves had less agency, and though there was a select group of radicals consistently advocating on their behalf, it was understood that their lives mattered less than everyone else's. I desperately want to declare that had I lived during those times, I would have been among the radicals. I haven't even been among the radicals of today who have been urgently calling for more compassion for those in bondage, or for an outright abolishment of prison.

"Around January, a dude was shooting ice and overdosed," James told me. "He had a lock on his door. By time they kicked his door in, he was stiff as a log."

Another time he watched a prisoner commit suicide.

"This white dude was telling his counselors he was going to kill himself, but they didn't believe him," James told me. "The next day, he stood on the top rock by the TVs and jump headfirst into the concrete. His brain hopped out his head like Jack-in-the-box. Dudes with phones recorded it and was sending it everywhere."

He said it was like a real live war, that lockdowns—no more than two showers a week, not much time outside of cramped cells—are instituted after every horrible incident, that the daily danger "is a riot can pop off and we're locked inside a building, and police don't come in unless they got two hundred officers. They will not run inside a building to save you, even if they see ten people on camera stabbing you."

"Death trap, man, that's why every day you have to be on point," he said. "I've seen damn near everything. These people don't care about us so...why lock us up? They don't give us nothing to do, so if we don't straighten up ourselves, it's detrimental. If you're not built right when you enter prison, you're going to be somebody's bitch or you're going to turn up [become extremely aggressive] to survive."

I've known this reality from a safe distance but, nonetheless, better than most Americans. You can't escape it when nearly half your brothers experience the wrong side of those walls and you spend much of your young life visiting prisons. I've known that though some of my brothers have done monstrous things, they are not monsters, that they can be just as loving and compassionate and wise as the rest of us, that they are just as complex and fully deserving of being treated like full human beings—that their lives matter—despite what they've done.

And yet too often I've had to fight the tendency to hate them the way so many who don't know them do, had to struggle to love them the way I know I'm supposed to. Too many days, I've noticed my thoughts about them becoming Fox News–like, imagining them as one-dimensional beings who deserve all the ugly visited upon them. Why should I care that James has been stabbed and subjected to witnessing suicides and murders? Wasn't he the one who drove that car during a crime that ended in a man's death? Didn't he get into fights and shoot-outs and high-speed chases? Didn't he sell the drugs that helped sink my hometown? Didn't he do other things I can only imagine? Weren't the actions I was aware of so disturbing they convinced me to limit the time my kids spent in my mother's St. Stephen home, which sometimes felt like a potential target for young men trying to hurt James?

★ ★ ★

Zadoc was thrown into a Berkeley County jail cell after sustaining multiple bites from a K-9 unit. The dog was let off his leash to attack after Zadoc, who was already handcuffed, smarted off at a police officer. He didn't receive treatment until Mama shamed officials. His injuries left him mostly bedridden and going back and forth to the hospital for weeks.

That was jail. In prison, he was stabbed "in the back and the face" during a fight and didn't receive treatment because neither he nor his opponent wanted to alert prison guards, knowing it would lead to lockdown time. He's now assumed guilty even when he's innocent when he comes across a St. Stephen police officer. I should care about that unfairness. But when I try, my mind reminds me that he led cops on multiple chases, earned a reputation as an unsavory character in St. Stephen, and spent time in that Baltimore prison where he was stabbed because troopers prevented him, James, and a friend from driving to New York to hurt people.

"What were you going to do with all those guns?" I asked Zadoc about their foiled New York trip.

"Get money," he said.

Every time I force myself to remember my little brothers' complex humanity, those stories and those questions flood my mind. Maybe that's why a letter from a Berkeley County jail from Jordan didn't move me much.

He detailed his disturbing life behind bars:

First thing I want you to know is I don't like to make Moms worry about me that's why I didn't say anything that day, 2 Sundays ago, the police lynch me. I was already on lock-up! Another inmate dash the police with defecation & urine, this happen after we ate dinner that Saturday. I was asking all night for someone to clean it up before breakfast, 'cuz they bring the cart with the food on it right through where the feces are. The police refuse to clean it & still brought breakfast, lunch through it. So since they refuse to clean it, I flooded my cell with water then let it out on the rock to flood the rock. Moments later they come in & cuff me to move me out so they can clean the cell. They cuffed me to the back bench with both of my hands cuff to the bench, the corporal walked past me, stop then started hitting me with her Walkie Talkie in my arm, neck and shoulder real hard. I couldn't do nothing but the good part is that all that was caught on camera. When they finished cleaning the room, they remove me off the bench to escort me back to the cell but when they got me in front of the door off the camera they all started beating me. Punching, kicking and kneeing me & hitting me with the Walkie Talkie. This went on for about 3 minutes until they allowed me to go in the cell. Also I've been on lock-up for over 14 days & haven't had a review hearing...They got me in the back where they only come around 3x's a day, no hour of re & unsanitary.

I found myself digesting those words first as a skeptical journalist, then as a fatigued brother, tired of talking about prison and thinking about prison and guards and fights and beatings and crime. But the claims deeper in the letter rang true.

Everyone from Mell [sic], *up to Sherrie they keep in touch & do for each other, but when it comes to me, Doc, and James it's like we the black sheep you feel me? I mean it's like everyone went off & forget South Carolina period, except Willie, he still do for Moms & Sherrie come through every now & then...I mean I know I'm here for what people assume I had something to do with, but at the same time I feel like in a time like this family suppose to stick/come together, I been here in the county for 2 years awaiting trial & it seems like everyone feels I already got life in prison, aint asking if I'm guilty, need a lawyer, if I need $ or nothing, it's like I'm dead to them already. I know it sounds crazy but that's how I see it. I'm not tripping though, I'm a man up regardless bruh.*

I found it difficult to empathize with Jordan even though I knew he had grown up during a period in which Mama and my stepfather had begun having problems and when James and Zadoc, the brothers closest to him, were dealing in drugs and guns.

The Georgia-Pacific wood plant, now just a hulking, hollowed-out, rusting monument to a dying industry, and other manufacturers were still hiring and employing thousands of people in our region when I was growing up, making life economically bearable for many, including the un- and undereducated. Jordan came along as the losses in the manufacturing and textile industries in the area had begun taking hold, increasing levels of poverty and instability, and crime. I never had to constantly adjust to upheaval and being shipped to different places in different states, like Jordan did, because of the instability at home.

Still, I empathized more with strangers than with my own brother. That's why I never visited Jordan as he awaited trial. Neither did I visit Zadoc or James or Smooch. I couldn't bear more prison visits. I spoke a good game publicly, frequently pulling out my "you don't have to be a monster to do something monstrous" line in speeches and forums and teachings about the importance of seeing the full complexity of deeply flawed men.

My struggle to remember to love my youngest brothers —while never excusing the things they've done—has been a schizophrenic endeavor. I'd remember all the calls about all the arrests. But then I'd scroll through my newsfeed to see that marijuana producers and sellers in Colorado generated $1.3 billion in revenue in 2016, while revenue was expected to top the one-billion-dollar mark in Washington in 2017—all legally, mostly without the violence that trailed those who tried to do the same where I grew up.

Then I'd remember that a man who bragged about casually sexually assaulting women—grabbing them by the pussy—a man who helped railroad five young black and Latino men in New York into false convictions, a man whose ex-wife once accused him of rape, was elevated by the American public to the highest elected position in the free world. Many of those who made Trump president would be among the first to condemn my brothers.

I'd remember the gobs of racial disparities that work against young black men in the prison and educational systems, heavily contributing to our overrepresentation in punitive institutions wrongly labeled "rehabilitation" centers. I'd remember the scores of men who have been wrongly convicted and freed, and many others who also have been but likely won't ever breathe free air again. I'd remember seeing the lynching postcards, the gaggle of smiling white faces standing at the feet of lifeless black bodies dangling from trees, and how almost none of them served a day for their crimes against humanity, a privilege that made it easier for the generations of their families to make their way in this country without the emotional, psychological, and all-too-real shackles that come with having loved ones imprisoned.

But then I'd remember Kim being shot to death and that bloody footprint. At family gatherings, I'd stare blankly and helplessly at nieces and nephews who had lost mothers and fathers to violence or prison, their lives almost derailed before they had a chance to really begin.

When I was a nine-year-old boy trying to digest how to respond to my hero going to prison, I simply stopped feeling. How to love a murderer without excusing the murder has always been a burning question in my brain. As a forty-five-year-old married father of two, I've found myself on the other end of the emotional scale. How to care again about the well-being of brothers who've done dastardly things that have made me angry and fearful and disgusted? How to hold fast to the belief that each of us deserves a second chance, to be loved?

As I stared at the photo of the bloody scene from James's prison dorm, I wondered what I would have felt if it was James on that floor. Would I have cried as much for him as I did when I received word that Damon had been killed?

★ ★ ★

Something Zadoc said convinced me not to give up on my youngest brothers. About a month before the twenty-fifth anniversary of Mr. Bunch's murder, Zadoc and I sat on Mama's front porch and talked about his life in a way we never had. We talked about what it meant that he was a two-year-old when Moochie went to prison, that he grew up in a household in flux and in survival mode. We were dealing with losing our hero and a primary breadwinner to prison. Mama was dealing with guilt and pain and anger and regret while wondering how she'd pay mounting monthly bills.

"My counselor told me that I was slowly dying," Mama said. "She said I had to be able to talk about it to be able to raise my other children. The faces of my children were saying, 'Mama, I need you, too.' When this thing happened to [Moochie], I think we all died some."

Crime research suggests that the younger a sibling is when an older sibling commits a violent crime, the more likely the criminal action will be repeated. It's their way of trying to connect with a family member they know they should love but who isn't there. Because of their age, they have fewer coping skills. Moochie was a convicted murderer, but the next seven siblings stayed free of serious crime. Zadoc broke that string. While experts may have theories about why that happens in families on this side of crime, Zadoc had a simpler explanation.

"That's what I wanted to do," he said. "It didn't matter about being good."

He grew up side by side with James and witnessed the parade of St. Stephen's most-desperate citizens in and out of our house. He didn't make excuses about why he did what he did, though I'm convinced the environment played a larger role than he understands. That's not how Zadoc helped me maintain empathy. It was something else he said.

"Real men go to prison," he told me as we sat on Mama's porch.

His words initially felt like a punch to the gut, an indictment of the path I had chosen, as though suggesting the rest of us had had it easy because we avoided prison. I thought it spoke of a dangerous mind-set, the kind I had heard propagated by gangsta rap songs, which reveled in violence and crime, glorified murder, and surviving drive-by shootings.

He wasn't bragging; he was explaining. To find yourself in a place designed to strip you of your humanity and come out sane on the other side takes a man, a *real man,* who can see and experience the worst and not lose himself and, sometimes, find himself at the bottom of the ugly. Though it took me years to realize it, that's what he was telling me. That's why Zadoc later married a woman with a solid military career. That's why they've spent the past several years building a life together, a stable home for their kids, away from the life he once lived. His story is at the same time a what-not-to-do warning for young black men, and a why-we-shouldn't-give-up reminder on those who've taken the wrong road.

Though that Zadoc-inspired revelation has stayed with me, kept me pushing for criminal justice reform and more resources for families like mine, there's a person in our family whose level of empathy for and advocacy of our wayward siblings surpasses everyone else's. He made an unexpected return home.

Freedom

On November 13, 2014, after more than thirty-two years of being handcuffed and shackled and suffering through solitary confinement, Moochie stepped off a bus in Charleston. If this feels like an abrupt way to introduce Moochie's new life of freedom to readers, it pales in comparison with how abrupt it felt to us when it happened. His unexpected bus trip was the thunder to the lightning of an unexpected decision from the parole board.

I first got word the board had approved his release while sitting on a couch in an apartment at Harvard University, where I was a 2014 Nieman Fellow, part of a program that invites twenty-four accomplished journalists from across the globe every year to study at the world's most recognizable university. I had long since given up hope Moochie would be free again. I had sworn off parole hearings; it was too hard to hold on to an always just-out-of-reach hope. Mama kept going and a couple of my brothers attended a few after I stopped.

"They gave Moochie parole!" the text read.

I reread it, then read it again and still couldn't get my brain to believe.

"Is this a sick joke?" I asked.

"No, it's true! Moochie is getting out," my sister Mel answered.

I was crying when Tracy walked into the room and sat down next to me and gently rubbed my back. We were at a particularly vulnerable time in our lives and marriage. I had recently been released from the hospital after a nearly two-week stay, having been diagnosed with the extremely rare autoimmune disease CIDP (chronic inflammatory demyelinating polyneuropathy). Just a few weeks before I got the text about Moochie, Tracy returned to the apartment after a short business trip to find me on the couch in a semiconscious state and got me to the emergency room. The disease, which had begun affecting me nearly six months earlier in the form of an inflamed neck and numb toes (at the time I didn't know they were symptoms), was full-blown. I didn't think I'd leave the hospital alive and told Tracy to find the life insurance policy. Tracy was upset I was there so long while a gaggle of doctors poked and probed me every way a man could be poked and probed. They thought I could be suffering from leukemia or another kind of cancer, or that bacteria had invaded my bloodstream, or that my heart had sustained a life-threatening level of damage.

Tracy was scared, looking at her once-strong husband lying helplessly in a hospital bed, and angry, because she thought the problem was obvious. I had developed a 104-degree fever that wouldn't break just a few days after I had received five consecutive days of intravenous treatment while sitting next to cancer patients with various wires protruding from their arms, too. The treatment, something called IVIG, was most likely the cause of the fever and subsequent blood clots that kept climbing higher in my legs.

For some reason doctors still can't explain, my immune system decided to attack the linings of my nerves, which began to shut them down and slowly robbed life from most of my large muscle groups. At about that time, I was attending a course at Harvard about brain development and health. It was there I learned people like me—those who had overcome a bevy of chronic stressors as children—were more susceptible to disease later in life, particularly in our forties and fifties. While outsiders marvel at our ability to be resilient in the face of overwhelming challenge, our bodies never forget. The stress we were able to stare down as kids, and find a way to end out on top anyway, may have fundamentally altered our bodies. Just as there is no definitive test that can determine how much the shock of watching Moochie be taken away to prison locked in my stutter, neither is there one to be certain that CIDP was able to afflict me because the PTSD that went undiagnosed in me for a quarter of a century had inflamed my nerves and slowly weakened them. But it is not crazy to suspect the link.

Before CIDP, I could run a 20-minute 5K, do 125 push-ups and 20 pull-ups. After the disease took hold, I had difficulty folding large towels, turning the switch on a lamp, had trouble walking and couldn't run—at all—and was too weak to stand on my toes. Tracy had to push me around in a wheelchair in the hospital during subsequent visits.

Willie and his wife, Ida, Sherrie, and my mother-in-law made the trip to Boston to help care for me; Josh and his wife sent me a check to help pay our bills; my fellow Niemans took turns grocery shopping and cooking and providing transportation for us and taking care of our kids. The low point was when Lyric, then a nine-year-old, ran to her room and hid in a closet after watching me struggle to make it to the bathroom with my right foot, where a blood clot had developed overnight, propped up on a wheeled desk chair.

"Daddy can't even walk," she sobbed softly as Tracy tried to soothe her.

That was the only thing that moved me; otherwise, I was numb. I wasn't afraid of dying; neither was I brave or upbeat. I did not send up prayers asking God to save or heal me. I was all prayed out. The faith I grew up with had not protected my family from Jim Crow and the racial discrimination and inequalities that came with it, and heavily contributed to the environment that increased the odds that my hero big brother would end up in prison. It had not protected me from a lifelong fight with a severe stutter that has shaped me more than anything else. It had not prevented the cycle of violence in my family that began with my maternal grandfather beating and shooting my grandmother and ended with my youngest brother in major trouble. That is if you don't count the violence visited upon my family during American chattel slavery, which we've traced back through Mama's familial line.

My family suffered from just about every malady imaginable, even though we've spent decades in the church. I had one living aunt by the time I got sick, because each of my other aunts and uncles had died in their fifties and sixties, or much younger. If God found it fit for them to die from a chronic illness, there was little reason to believe I should, or would, be spared. I was not in a mood to pretend that a "laying on of hands" would cure me. Besides that, all those years we spent praying for Moochie's release had gone unanswered. And his new faith, Rastafarianism, seemed to make his journey in prison harder, given that the dreadlocks he grew as a sign of spiritual commitment had been a primary reason he had been initially denied parole.

A gaggle of members from a church I used to attend set up a prayer chain for me, sending good vibes and well-wishes to the Cambridge hospital where I was stuck in bed. My former pastor from the Myrtle Beach area contacted a pastor he knew in Boston and had him stop by the hospital to pray with Tracy and offered to counsel us. Those were sincere gestures from people trying to love me from afar. I had left that church—a conservative, mostly white, evangelical church—after I could no longer stomach a racial hatred too many in the congregation had developed after Barack Obama was elected in 2008. I can't tell you what percentage of the church's members voted for Donald Trump and his open bigotry in 2016, but it wouldn't surprise me if it matched the 70 percent who voted for him in the county where we lived.

They would tell you that I'm wrong or exaggerating or unfairly misreading their intentions, that their horrific response to the election of the nation's first black president had nothing to do with race. I have no doubt they sincerely believe that. Still, I have no doubt it was about race and a hatred more based in fear than grounded in animus, but a racial hatred nonetheless.

I initially tried to steer the white people I knew away from that response. When they accidentally copied me onto ugly email chains, I'd gently tell them why that was out of bounds instead of scolding them. I was committed to that church. It was where my kids were dedicated, my wife and I were baptized, and I wrote a check giving away the last five hundred dollars in our bank account because I believed God wanted me to, even though Tracy and I were struggling so much we could hardly afford gas when it was still little more than a dollar per gallon.

When church members kept forwarding those email chains and kept saying and believing things that grew uglier by the week, I stopped trying. That was after I had already been removed from teaching in the kids' church because several members had grown uncomfortable with my advocacy for LGBT equality and support of Obama. This was in a church I convinced my wife to join because I met the white pastor when we both were part of a community outreach effort to bridge racial divides in the South. He was open about his past racism and how he believed God had called him to make amends, which is why he knocked on the door of every black house in the neighborhood when he founded his church, inviting them to join. Some did.

He's not racist, and neither are the white members of his congregation who have a disdain for Obama and, though they would deny it, black people like me. It's a form of cognitive dissonance too often mistaken for racism by those who haven't lived in the South long enough to understand the nuance of how race is experienced in the region. For too many members of my former church, we don't fit the stereotype of black people they unknowingly carry in their brains. We are educated and "well-spoken." We got married and *then* had kids. We work hard. We don't make excuses. We don't rely upon food stamps and are not on welfare. Influential people are interested in what we say.

That's why they are angry when black people like me and Tracy and President Obama and Michelle Obama—whose ancestors were enslaved not too far from where I grew up—refuse to pretend that racism is a small problem in twenty-first-century America. They want me to say that other black people who haven't made it have squandered opportunities and don't deserve empathy. They want me to emphasize the good decisions I made and downplay the help I received—food stamps; free lunch at school and during the summer in my youth; free government cheese and beans; unearned breaks and second chances from caring teachers and strange adults; a free science and technology summer program at Claflin College (now Claflin University); an invitation to the 1990 South Carolina Governor's School that padded my high school resume; Pell grants in college; a loan a (white) Bank of America executive told his bank to give me even though I wasn't financially qualified; a strong, stubborn mother and brilliant older siblings; and numerous publicly funded programs

I began benefiting from before I was old enough to go to kindergarten.

I faced enormous challenges and didn't come out unscathed, but also received countless handouts and hand-ups that helped steer me toward Davidson and Harvard and away from the path Moochie blazed. Check my criminal history and you'll find no infractions more serious than speeding tickets. That doesn't mean I never stole—I have—or never lied—I have—or cheated—I have. It means I was fortunate that the arrestable acts I committed while growing up never landed me behind bars.

I was gifted with the kind of personality ideally suited for the environment and unique struggles I faced. Academic work came easily to me, often even when I didn't work hard. I came out on the other side of CIDP better than many other patients in part because I had been blessed with a healthy body and more muscle mass than the average man.

It's true I had a hand in my success. I worked hard (mostly). I made wise decisions (often, not always). I was stubborn as hell when I needed to be stubborn as hell. I listened when I needed to learn, taught when it was time to speak. Don't be fooled, though; I'm no self-made man. I needed help—a lot of help—and got just enough. For a variety of reasons, too many other young black men and women who faced what I faced were deprived of the assistance they needed, including a few members of my family, and have been vilified and stereotyped by those claiming to love all God's children. That's the difference between me and them.

Many of the people I left behind in that church don't want me to tell my story that way, because they know they can't simply write off my words as those of the lazy and embittered. That's why they embrace the likes of Tim Scott, the first black elected senator from the Deep South since Reconstruction, and Clarence Thomas, black men who've also successfully navigated the minefield that is Southern racism, come out on top, and either preach an up-by-the-bootstraps kind of politics, don't spend much time reminding white Southerners about pervasive discrimination, or say it gently when they do.

That's why I know many members of my former church were open to embracing someone like Trump long before Trump came along, not because they are racist, but because defeating racism is often not a priority for them. Their tolerance for the fight includes interracial prayer groups, dinners, and cookouts, and preaching that God loves everyone. They will volunteer to help young black kids read, launch prison ministries, and take in black foster kids. My former white pastor rapped a sermon with a young black teenager, supported the creation of a black choir, and made space for me to teach a bit about implicit bias. Even today, years after I left the church, I can call up just about any member—including everyone who voted for Trump—and they'd show up in the middle of the night and help me and my family if I asked.

That's why when they declare they are not racist, they should be believed. The problem is that they support policies and politicians that clearly hurt people of color anyway. They are okay with voter suppression disguised as voter ID laws. They aren't bothered enough by the high level of mass incarceration and the racial imbalance found within our prisons, despite their prison ministries. They harshly judge black people they see in a Walmart buying a steak or soda with an EBT card. They are as likely to believe the link between violence and dark skin as the nearest white nationalist, which is why they were quick to defend George Zimmerman when he killed Trayvon Martin.

They don't understand—and don't seem to want to—the effects of toxic stress on a poverty-stricken young brain and what that means for behavior in school and a student's prospects afterwards. They are sympathetic and cling to an overly sanitized version of law enforcement and law and order, no matter how many young black men and women are killed by police or brutalized in prison. (I've also had white progressive friends and colleagues get upset and call me radical when I argued that a cop's fear is not a good reason to shoot an unarmed black man.) They would be unmoved if I told them about the findings of a major study published by the Marshall Project in 2017, which found that a white person's killing of a black man is eight times more likely to be ruled justified than other kinds of killings, no matter the circumstance, and that a black person's killing of a white person is almost never considered legally warranted. They'd immediately begin ticking off reasons all those black men were at fault rather than consider the chilling implications of such a finding—that the once seemingly crazy rantings of Prison Moochie, about the depths of racism in America, weren't that far off the mark.

Their view of Southern history includes the most sympathetic view of the Confederacy in the country. Black protest, peaceful or angry, turns them off, no matter how legitimate, no matter how serious the grievances. Small talk and smiles with black colleagues and neighbors convince them things aren't too bad and help persuade them to ignore racial inequalities. When their black friends aren't screaming, they take it as evidence everything is fine. When their black friends decide to scream, their black friends must just be too sensitive and need to get over the past.

They are neither racist, nor allies. Oftentimes, they are the biggest hurdles black people must clear along the path of racial progress because they frequently prioritize their feelings and thirst for comfort above all else. They've convinced themselves that white people being falsely accused of racism is a bigger offense than an unarmed black man being shot five times in the back by a police officer, which happened in North Charleston, the city I spent my youth visiting to catch the latest movie on the silver screen or hang out in the mall, or being choked to death for selling loose cigarettes the way Eric Garner was in New York.

They will eagerly intervene with God on my behalf to cure my body. But when it comes to doing the difficult work of dismantling structures and procedures that keep institutionalized racism alive, they are often a hindrance. It's easy to fight the unrepentant David Duke, much harder to stand against the white person who helped change your kids' diapers and hugged you after an emotional church service. God, how I wish it was true that only racists voted for Trump, the man who Duke said echoed everything that former head of the KKK had been preaching all his life. He could not win with their vote alone. The racist Trump vote was only effective because nearly 60 percent of white American voters—he won the white vote at every economic level, not just the white poor and working-class—chose Trump despite his open bigotry. That's a devastating commentary about twenty-first-century America.

The more I began understanding that reality, the more I began realizing Moochie's persistent talk of black love and black uplift and white supremacy wasn't that crazy after all, that I should have been listening more closely to him instead of trying to teach him to ignore the racial ugliness in this country I didn't want to fully acknowledge. Racism is as insidious and as rooted into our culture as he had been trying to tell me all those years in all those letters and prison visits, just not the way he envisioned.

Much of it is not purposeful, though the damage cuts just as deep. That point was further driven home when I took a course taught by the famed historian Skip Gates at Harvard, who shared that he's had white colleagues, some of the most learned men in the world, doubt his claims about technological and other advances made by long-ago Africans. It made me realize I wasn't the only accomplished black professional who has had his sanity and seriousness questioned by well-meaning white colleagues who—because they didn't know what we knew about race and refused to learn—assumed we had to be wrong or exaggerating what we were experiencing. I had grown sick and tired of being sick and tired of former church members and former white colleagues who repeatedly tried to steer me away from uncomfortable discussions about race, no matter how gently or expertly or empathetically I approached the subject.

That was my state of mind when the text about Moochie's parole came in; my blinders had been removed about my faith, about race. That's also why I never thought that day would come. I had given up hope.

"What's wrong?" Tracy asked as I cried on the couch.

I couldn't answer, just showed her the text. Moochie was coming home. I still can't explain why. He had cut his dreadlocks years earlier but wasn't released then. Sometime between 2005 and 2014, the Bunch family stopped petitioning to keep him locked up. Mr. Bunch's sisters spoke to me in 2005 but did not want to speak with anyone from my family, or me, again. I've honored that request and always will, despite my lingering questions, though it wouldn't surprise me if they showed my oldest brother mercy.

We wanted to be the first faces he saw as he walked out of the prison's doors, but no one could tell us when he would be released. A correctional official visited Mama's house to ensure it was suitable for Moochie and I called my contacts in the department, to no avail. It would take a few months until he finished his reorientation classes, was the last thing they said until a couple of weeks later when Moochie borrowed a cell phone from a fellow passenger on a Greyhound bus to tell us he was free.

By that day, he was years removed from solitary confinement; his mental health had improved greatly, and was further restored by a program called the Better Living Incentive Community, or BLIC. A warden in South Carolina named Michael Mann decided the get-tough approach wasn't working. Giving prisoners freedom rather than harsh punishments might more likely change behavior, he thought. Mann began his experiment not in a juvenile or minimum-security facility, but at Lee Correctional, the state's largest maximum-security prison, one that houses the most violent offenders. It's where James and Moochie crossed paths inside, though James declined an offer to become a cellmate with his older brother.

Moochie made it through a long waiting list and was accepted into BLIC. Prisoners take and teach dozens of betterment courses, including painting, musical instruments (classical and otherwise), biblical Greek, barbering, and CDL licensing, among others. There are also rotating game and movie nights every weekend. Moochie took carpentry and electricity and for the first time in decades truly felt like a full man. Prisoners were free to roam until 11:30 p.m. on weekdays, a little later on weekends. In non-BLIC dorms, prisoners were in their cells from about 6:00 p.m. to 6:30 a.m., "locked down in there with your cellmate regardless if y'all get along or not. Y'all stuck in this little spot about the size of a bathroom."

It's the kind of progress that gives me hope, makes me think real reform is possible, that maybe all the ways the system had neglected to consider the fate of families, and the violent convicts they love, might be reconsidered. Several Republican officials in Southern states and elsewhere in recent years had been leading reform efforts that have saved those states money by slowing, or in some cases, reversing the growing incarceration rate. Federal efforts had been taking off as well during the Obama era under Attorney General Eric Holder. Trump's election has threatened that progress, something else white Trump voters don't want to be held accountable for, no matter the damage such a reversal will once again cause families like mine.

Of course we want victims to get justice. Of course we want people to pay for their misdeeds. We just want men like Moochie, who have served their time and found a way to maintain their humanity through it all, to be given a chance to make amends and be allowed to do some good in the world.

★ ★ ★

A few days after Moochie's release, several members of our family met at a restaurant. We hugged for a long time. He was thrilled to see that Tracy had grown dreadlocks, as had Lyric. He found out later Aunt Doretha and her daughter and granddaughters had them, too.

"Power, power, that's power," he kept saying, rubbing his hair. We didn't tell him that Tracy and our daughter grew dreads because Tracy was tired of spending so much time and money at the hairdresser. (Tracy later cut her hair, as did my aunt and cousin Catherine.)

Mostly, he just sat there at the head of the table, as in the eye of a hurricane, the world around him new and old at once. Around him, his family members made plans to run a half marathon in Myrtle Beach—Moochie would run it, too, chatting up every person he would meet along the 13.1-mile path like a baby-kissing politician in a tight race—joked about Duke-UNC basketball and the Dallas Cowboys. Younger siblings wondered aloud what to do with him, talked of securing him a driver's license and a job and the need to be patient and to learn about *real* life, not that alternative reality he developed in prison.

His name? Mtume Obalaji Mfume? Herbert Lee Bailey? Moochie? On that day, in that moment, I'm not entirely sure. I'm not sure he knew. That's why I was scared for him in a way I wasn't when he was behind bars. I didn't want him to be in prison any more than he wanted to. But I knew he mastered how to cope in that hell. He knew little of the world he had just reentered. The racial disparities he faced as a twenty-two-year-old in the heart of the Deep South had not disappeared when he returned as a fifty-four-year-old man.

The Christian Knights of the Ku Klux Klan, which was still marching through small towns and cities in South Carolina long after he left the world, had been replaced by a discrimination harder to define, making it harder to root out. The world into which he returned is one in which a white man without a high school diploma is often more employable than a black man with a bachelor's degree, a white man with a criminal record more desirable than a black man who avoided the prison industrial complex, a world in which a black-sounding name on a resume makes potential employers balk.

He came back into a world that punishes people for having been punished, one in which fear scares up votes and perpetrators of violent crime are forever defined by that act, no matter how long ago it was committed or the context in which it occurred, no matter if they've changed or paid dearly for their mistake. They are such pariahs they—and their families—are left out of discussions about ways to reduce our overly large prison population.

He came back into this world not totally clear of his old one. His release came with five years of probation and a strict warning to show up to every meeting with his parole officer, abstain from drugs, and keep up with his parole fees. To me, it felt as though he had been released from a cage but put on a leash. To him, it was bliss.

"Man, for the first couple of nights, I was afraid to go to sleep," he told me. "I didn't want to wake up and find out it was just a dream."

Sometimes he would wake up in the middle of the night, kicking and screaming in bed, flashing back to what he faced in prison. He, too, would be diagnosed with PTSD.

★ ★ ★

About eight months after his release, Moochie spoke with a fellow ex-prisoner who had guided him in his faith and had been doing the same for countless other prisoners. Moochie wanted to go back to prison, to mentor those still incarcerated. It would take a while to make that happen, but we headed back to prison together to retrace some of the miles the family had traveled all those years earlier to see Moochie in prison. I wanted to see if the ride to Ridgeville would feel different with him in the car.

On those back roads, we were greeted by a large, handmade sign reading "Your sins killed Jesus" amid the pine forests and small barns. It spoke volumes. I only recently began noticing the sign. Or maybe its message grabbed me for the first time or in a new way: the tenuous connection of the sins of one condemning another, an almost celebratory, bedrock belief, not only of the Southern form of Christianity, but of America's justice system.

That sign's message, the allusion that evil must be punished or the cosmic order will be disturbed, that the Jesus who died for us will return as an avenging super warrior, is the ultimate salve to those who have been unjustly harmed. There is no balm for those unjustly harmed on the other side of crime—the criminal's family, who are often ignored, shunned, or viewed as unindicted co-conspirators. There is no lecture you can attend or book you can peruse to fully understand their plight. How I wish my family and I didn't know.

We learned that prison isn't just steel bars and razor wire fencing, guards and tiny windowless cells and black men and white toilets. It's not just the ever-present, faint smell of urine, sweat, and Clorox bleach. It's what you think and how you think and how you see what you see. It's every waking moment and more than a few that pass by in your dreams. It is how you talk and how you hide a vital part of yourself in plain sight for fear of being found out.

There is no praying your way out of it, no succeeding your way out of it, no leaving it behind. It infects your behavior in ways subtle and not, seeps into your subconscious and refuses to leave. That's true even if you are never subject to an invasive pat-down and strip search and never feel the cold of steel wrapped around your wrists. Prison isn't a place you send a man; it's what you do to his family, and what his family eventually does to society.

Jody joined us on the ride to Ridgeville, the place where Volvo is building its first American manufacturing plant in a region that has bled such jobs for a quarter of a century. Growing up, we knew Ridgeville for two things: Lieber and MacDougall Correctional Institutions. According to prison records, Moochie spent time in those prisons in 1986 and 1987. I would have been about fourteen, a little younger than my son, Kyle—who has never visited a prison. I can't remember if we still owned a wood-paneled station wagon by then or had upgraded to a large brown family van.

Pine forests and Spanish moss–draped live oaks guided us along the way. Carter's combination gas station–Chinatown restaurant greeted us in Ridgeville, as did gated private estates with two- and three-story brick and ranch-style homes with yards too large for a push lawn mower, and a few gated communities and cornfields and countless churches and rows of barns and new and rusted farm equipment dotting a windy, two-lane paved road. There were railroad tracks and a four-way stop—two paved roads, two dirt roads—a mile from the redbrick Bethel A.M.E., a cemetery and two broken basketball goals. A water tower hovered over it all.

It was quiet, the kind of place you wouldn't mind getting lost in, knowing that strangers would invite you into their homes for a meal if the few public eating establishments were closed. It was beautiful, something I hadn't noticed during all those trips to Lieber. Moochie seemed proud that he and two of his brothers were taking a trip together for the first time in more than three decades. I didn't speak much as I drove, only listening to my never-shy brothers debate about the best way to move the family forward together.

We took a left onto Wilborn Avenue and past a redbrick sign that read "Lieber Correctional Institution." We pulled into a white gravel rock parking lot, the Ford Taurus pointed toward the prison and its razor wire and rusted exterior.

"We made it," I said, not knowing what else to say.

"Hey, man, I don't know if we should park," Moochie said quickly. "They might get suspicious. They might think we doin' something we ain't supposed to. Let's go."

I switched the car's ignition back on. We headed back to his place, a modest cinder block house Mama had secured for him and a girlfriend. It was there he told me about his attempts to slowly integrate into a twenty-first-century world he had never known—about staying on his parole officer's good side, about how he wanted to teach, about his attempts to secure work, even if it was part-time and spotty, about doing absolutely nothing that could send him back to prison.

He ever-so-gently asked for a few dollars. I slipped him two twenty-dollar bills.

"Boy, without family, I don't know what I would do," he said as he pocketed the money.

As we spoke, his gaze rarely left his reflection in a mirror in the bathroom. He was tending to his salt-and-pepper hair. The beginnings of dreadlocks were already reemerging.

Epilogue

Imagine a white man was born in America in 1946, about four years after my black mother, about two decades before the Civil Rights Movement forced the signing of the Civil Rights Act. Imagine he was rich beyond belief before he breathed his first breath, so wealthy he could breezily describe a multimillion-dollar gift from his daddy as a "small" loan.

Now imagine he used that fortunate beginning—he was rubbing elbows with the most influential families in the world's most famous city, New York, while my mother was being forced into a marriage at age thirteen to a much older man who would beat her—to discriminate so comprehensively against black people he would get sued twice by the Justice Department. Imagine him using his privileged perch to help railroad five young black and brown boys into prison sentences for a rape they did not commit (even though he would be accused of rape by an ex-wife before she softened her language). Imagine he reportedly said he believed blacks had a lazy trait and had black employees ushered into the background when he showed up at one of his properties; and imagine he lead a bigoted movement fueled by a conspiracy theory about the birthplace of the country's first black president; and kicked off his own presidential campaign by labeling most immigrants from Mexico as rapists and murderers; and spoke glowingly of a fictional story about Muslims being mowed down by bullets dipped in pig's blood; and proposed banning Muslims from entering the United States; and claimed a federal judge was not worthy of overseeing a case against him because the judge is "Mexican"; and declared that black people live in Hell. Imagine he encouraged violent supporters at his rallies—by promising to pay their legal fines—or initially excused two white men in Boston who beat a homeless Hispanic man in his name, then later recanted. Imagine he hired a man who bragged that he provided the platform for the alt-right (read: white nationalists) and earned a ringing endorsement from the country's best-known white supremacist while giving other white supremacists wet dreams.

Imagine that white man—who was attending posh private schools when my black mother was picking cotton and tobacco to help her family make ends meet in a town where black people felt afraid to be outside after dark—squandered his millions, and his companies filed for bankruptcy multiple times. Imagine the businesses he led did not perform as well as competitors, that he was accused of sexual assault and harassment by various women over many years and was caught fleecing millions of dollars from working, middle-class Americans through a phony university and a refusal to pay his debts, and after all of that was rewarded with the presidency of the most powerful nation on the planet because a majority of white people from every socioeconomic background chose him.

It's the kind of caricature of the United States that would arise from the imaginings of my oldest brother, Moochie, when his brain was still affected by years of solitary confinement, when he would write "AmeriKKKa" in his letters to family members. And yet, that's the world Moochie was released back into after more than three decades behind bars. Since he was freed in 2014, multiple police officers have either gone uncharged or been acquitted in horrific events that ended in the death or debasement of black people, including Freddie Gray in Baltimore, who had his spinal cord nearly severed at the neck while in police custody; and Walter Scott, shot five times while running away—caught on video—by a cop in North Charleston who would secure a hung jury in the state prosecution against him (he's in prison after taking a deal before an anticipated federal trial); and Philando Castile in Minnesota, executed after a traffic stop even though he calmly told the officer he was legally carrying a firearm; or Charnesia Corley, who said she was digitally penetrated in a gas station parking lot by police in Texas searching for drugs in her vagina after they stopped her for a few minor traffic violations.

In the days I was finishing up the final edits for this book, Andrew Cohen of the Brennan Center at New York University School of Law released a report documenting a case in which a white juror said he voted to send a black man to death row because that black man was a nigger.

"Mr. [Barney] Gattie expressed his feelings about the case in general," Cohen wrote. "He stated that there are two kinds of black people in the world—'regular black folks' and 'niggers.' Mr. Gattie noted that he understood that some people do not like the word 'nigger' but that is just what they are, and he 'tells it like he sees it.'"

The victim was from one of the "good black families," which is what convinced Gattie to vote in favor of the death penalty. Had the victim been just another nigger, like the man convicted of killing her, Gattie would not have voted for death because he didn't care much for niggers. Did prosecutors get this new information and immediately join the defense to petition a judge for a new trial, or a commutation of the sentence? Did they say, even if the defendant is guilty, the American justice system simply cannot abide cosigning on such blatant racism, that true justice can't be based on such ugliness? Of course not. Instead, prosecutors immediately went to Gattie to get him to sign a new affidavit to nullify what he told the investigators.

"Gattie, who now swore he wasn't a bigot, claimed he had been drinking beer and whiskey when he spoke to the defense, and didn't pay much attention when the affidavit was read to him," Cohen wrote. "He said many of his statements 'were taken out of context and simply not accurate.' He signed the defense affidavit because he 'just wanted to get rid of them.' That second affidavit, the one in which Gattie—who is deceased—swore he had no racial animus, has been the basis of the state's defense for the past 20 years."

The week the Cohen piece was published, we learned that yet another police officer was found not guilty in the killing of yet another young black dude. Jason Stockley, who was a St. Louis police officer in 2011 when he shot Anthony Lamar Smith four times after a car chase, did nothing wrong, according to our justice system. The judge who acquitted the former cop delivered an acquittal even though Stockley's voice was captured on police radio saying he was going to kill that "motherfucker" during the chase—before proceeding to kill Smith. Stockley, prosecutors said, planted a gun on Smith to make the shooting seem like self-defense.

Why did Judge Timothy Wilson look at that damning evidence, knowing an internal affairs and FBI investigation led to the charges against Stockley, then set Stockley free anyway? In his thirty years on the bench, Wilson wrote, "an urban drug dealer not in possession of a firearm would be an anomaly." Never mind that only Stockley's DNA was on the gun, and that it was against protocol for an officer involved in a shooting to climb into a vehicle where he had just killed a man, giving him plenty of time and opportunity to plant a gun while other officers secured the area and moved Smith's body. Never mind that Stockley admitted to having unauthorized weapons. That Stockley said he was going to kill Smith before killing Smith? It was a high-stress situation and such words can be taken out of context, the judge concluded. The judge should have just said that Smith was a "nigger"—a drug dealer like my younger brothers—and not a "good black," and because of that, no amount of evidence would ever be enough to send a cop to prison for murdering such a man.

I didn't want to be angry while writing this book, but the cases out of Georgia and St. Louis, and so many before them—in addition to hearing about a sheriff in Louisiana who voiced opposition to prison reform because it would mean the "good" prisoners who provided free labor for the state were going to be released—made that difficult. A decision by Harvard University, the place I spent a year studying, providing me a leg up in my career, made that impossible. Harvard refused to admit a woman named Michelle Jones, though she was a widely sought-after historian who had been accepted just about everywhere she had applied. She enrolled in NYU. Given what she has overcome, she will be fine. But she wanted Harvard. And Harvard chose her, too, declaring she was "one of the strongest candidates in the country last year, period."

Then it said no.

Jones had served twenty years in prison for killing her own child. She told Harvard about the crime and her prison sentence but, according to a couple of officials, didn't fully explain what happened and minimized her crime "to the point of misrepresentation." That seems like little more than a fig leaf of a rationale, particularly given what one of the two professors who flagged her application said.

"We didn't have some preconceived idea about crucifying Michelle," John Stauffer, one of those American studies professors, told the Marshall Project. "But frankly, we knew that anyone could just punch her crime into Google, and Fox News would probably say that P.C. liberal Harvard gave 200 grand of funding to a child murderer, who also happened to be a minority. I mean, c'mon."

She killed her own baby. Of course that makes her one of the "niggers." Right?

Moochie left the world in 1982 and reentered it thirty-two years later. Since he has been free, the American justice system has said it was perfectly okay that a blatantly racist white man helped send a black man to death row and that a police officer could shoot a black man five times after saying he was going to do just that, while a university I have come to admire told a woman that she could not seek redemption there because those who toss around black pathology like a deflated football might use it to criticize them.

None of these cases is an anomaly. Race is routinely used to send black men to prison, or to death, even though the justice system and Supreme Court frequently pretend race plays little to no role. Police officers are routinely found not guilty—that is if they face charges at all—no matter their egregious actions during the killing of black men, and others. Those who say they believe in redemption, and want to facilitate that redemption, frequently renege on that promise when pressured by those who don't want black people who have done awful things to have a chance to become known for more than their worst act.

I grew up in the American South. Long ago I became accustomed to routine, friendly interactions with white Southerners who were quick to pray for black souls but slow to mobilize to protect black bodies if it meant challenging a system in which badges and batons made those wearing them as untouchable as those wearing crosses and carrying holy water. That's why Harvard's decision about Michelle Jones cut deepest. Because it's Harvard, a place that prides itself on leading and transforming the world, even when it's hard—especially when it's hard. Because it sends an ugly message, that even the most powerful white allies can be cowed to leave people like Jones and my family behind. It says we are too toxic, unworthy of their full embrace. It says we will forever be unforgiven.

That message couldn't come at a worse time, given that black Americans and other people of color are forced to watch in horror as the tens of millions of white Americans who voted to send Trump and his transparent, transactional bigotry to Washington still proudly embrace him while fiercely defending statues in the public square that celebrate men who lynched and murdered in the name of a racism that was as much a foundational tenet of this country as the idea that all men were created equal. Be a black man or woman and commit a grave sin, be defined as a monster. Be a rich white dude and commit many sins, be welcomed into the White House. While many Trump fans are doubling down, many white liberals seem as concerned with telling black people to protest neither too loudly nor too angrily as they are with fighting bigotry itself. It doesn't give me hope that when the toughest decisions must be made—true criminal justice reform can't happen without contending with the reality of families like mine—they'll be on our side.

By the way, Michelle Jones found herself pregnant after a "nonconsensual" sex act when she was fourteen. Her mother beat her with a board in her stomach after finding out. Jones found herself in a series of foster and group homes after that beating. Yes, she did a horrible thing and had to suffer the consequences. But when will society be made to answer for its treatment of her during her formative years?

She had a psychological breakdown "after years of abandonment and domestic violence, and inflicted similar treatment on her own son, Brandon Sims." The boy died in 1992 under still murky circumstances. Jones, during a stay at a mental-health crisis center, admitted to burying him without notifying police. A former friend testified against her, saying Jones confessed to "having beaten the boy and then leaving him alone for days in their apartment, eventually returning to find him dead in his bedroom." That's why she went to prison, not because she is an uncaring sociopath expert in the art of killing.

In twenty-first-century America, Harvard couldn't stomach a black woman who had paid a dear price for an awful crime and had risen above it all, even as America found a way to stomach Donald Trump as president of the United States. He's in the Oval Office because 57 percent of white American voters decided that he should lead us, despite all the ugly he has said, done, and proposed and because they are quick to provide men like him second and third chances even while not caring, or not caring enough, about the harsh origins of people like Michelle Jones and Mama and Moochie.

I'm not arguing that black people who do awful things should be excused because they had it hard. Society could neither survive nor thrive under such circumstances. I'm arguing that their background should be taken into account when considering their treatment at the hands of the justice system, and not only for them, but for their already-vulnerable families. I'm arguing that vengeance is not an effective way to seek or achieve true justice.

I've learned that "good black people" like me must more forcefully emphasize that truth, and do it unapologetically. And there are a lot of "good black people" in my family. I interviewed the nation's first black president and had governors and congressmen and multimillionaires on speed dial and have had my byline in several dozen newspapers and magazines. I have a brother who owns a couple of fitness centers in the D.C. area, having established them after spending years as an air traffic controller; a younger brother who helped build some of the trucks used in the *Transformers* movies, has been married longer than I have, and put two kids through college, with another who was so accomplished she graduated high school early; and a brother who used to take companies public and now manages his daughters' highly successful singing and acting careers. The Bailey family was well represented on the entertainment stage and in the crowd at one of the last big White House events during the Obama era. (I only later got to see photos of young cousins smiling next to Michelle Obama, because I was working and couldn't make it.)

I have nieces and nephews whose academic credentials are more impressive than mine. We've received degrees from or studied at some of the nation's top colleges and universities. My youngest sister is a stage actress, entrepreneur, and IT professional; my oldest sister has worked for Delta Air Lines for several years. A young cousin recently got promoted to captain in the U.S. Army. Cousins who feel like siblings have taken care of their families—and sometimes me—and worked twelve-hour shifts in factories for decades with little complaint and have long provided light no matter how dark things got in our small Southern town. A brother has been making waves for years trying to establish a nonprofit to help the dregs of society the way our mother did. And I'm married to a woman who earned a doctorate and am the father of two kids I fully expect to surpass me in every way that matters because they are just that bright and brilliant and beautiful.

The sacrifices made, and the challenges faced, by those in the generation before mine were not made in vain. Because they survived, because Aunt Doretha kept her dignity and calm and thirst for excellence alive while cleaning the diapers of white babies and navigating a North that wasn't as racially equal as too many pretend, because Mama moved mountains, many of us have tasted the kind of success those who came before us were capable of attaining had they lived in a different country at a different time. You can read these words because of them maybe more than me. While my family has too often felt like the black sheep of the black sheep because of the ugly things done by some within our ranks, we've produced our fair share of American Dream stories. Given our origins, it's fair to say we've done more good than should have been expected, and plan to do even more.

Still, I've learned that *good* black people like me are a flip of the coin from being considered one of the niggers, and often are considered such despite our accomplishments and no matter how many times we appease white people who prioritize their own feelings and comfort over the often messy fight for racial equality. If we argue too passionately for the possibility of redemption for the wayward in our ranks or refuse to accept the nonsensical premise that because some of us made it through a gauntlet of challenge, each of us should have, or if we don't go along with the color-blind myth or insist upon proportionate punishment, we are quickly labeled race hustlers and race baiters and the racially obsessed. Niggers.

I've learned that it is not a stretch to believe that had I been born first, not fifth, it would have been one of my brothers crying on a couch reading a text about me unexpectedly receiving parole after more than three decades instead of the other way around. That's why I know that if I don't love Moochie—and my sisters and broken aunts and uncles and my younger brothers and cousins and my parents and so many other black families like ours—I can't fully love myself.

And I plan to start loving myself fully.

Acknowledgments

I'm not a self-made man. I owe debts I'll never be able to repay to countless people. I know many of their names but have forgotten others, though not the impact they had on me as a boy and now as a man. This book would not have happened if not for each of them, including Judith Gurewich and the good folks at Other Press, my literary agent, Leah Spiro of Riverside Creative Management, and the Open Society Foundations, though this is far from an exhaustive list.

James Rosen of McClatchy followed my work in Myrtle Beach while he was in the nation's capital and helped open doors. Tim Golden, formerly of *The Washington Post,* and Bill Keller, now with The Marshall Project and formerly of *The New York Times,* helped usher this story onto the national stage. Lori Kelly, Kei Sullivan, Carolyn Murray, Patricia O'Connor, Gwen Fowler, Mike and Janet Morgan, Dawn Bryant, David Wren, Maya Prabhu, Lisa Fleisher, Paula Ellis, Jeffry Couch, John X. Miller, Mona Prufer, Melinda Waldrop, Johanna Wilson, Mary Hitt McCoy, Keith Jacobs, along with so many other colleagues I had at *The Sun News,* were vital in my development as a journalist. Cliff Harrington and Bob Meadows of *The Charlotte Observer* helped launch my career, as did Bill Giduz of Davidson College. Cole Barton and Ruth Ault were among my most influential professors. Friends such as Ginny and Greg Kintz and Sally Hare and Jim Rogers provided me focus and helped steel my spine. The honesty of men such as Joe Moglia, now of Coastal Carolina University, formerly of Wall Street fame, has inspired me.

I also must thank Ann Marie Lipinski, the rest of the crew at the Nieman Foundation, and my fellow 2014 Nieman fellows. Without them, my life would be much different—and not for the better—for so many reasons.

Then there's my family, including members mentioned elsewhere in this book, and those not. I would not have survived long enough to tell this story, and so many others, without each of you.

My daughter, Lyric Grace Bailey, has taught me to keep seeking truth and become a better human being. My son, Kyle Joshua Bailey, forced me to see the world with new eyes, without which I would be lost.

My wife, Dr. Tracy Lashawn Swinton Bailey, is my everything.

ISSAC J. BAILEY was born in St. Stephen, South Carolina, and holds a degree in psychology from Davidson College in North Carolina. Having trained at the prestigious Poynter Institute for journalists in St. Petersburg, Florida, he has been a professional journalist for twenty years. He has taught applied ethics at Coastal Carolina University and, as a Nieman Fellow, has taught journalism at Harvard Summer School. Bailey has won numerous national, state, and local awards for his writings. He currently lives in Myrtle Beach with his wife and children.